First World War

and Army of Occupation

War Diary

France, Belgium and Germany

19 DIVISION
58 Infantry Brigade,
Brigade Machine Gun Company
1 March 1916 - 28 February 1918

WO95/2093/3

The Naval & Military Press Ltd
www.nmarchive.com
Published in association with The National Archives

Published by

The Naval & Military Press Ltd

Unit 10 Ridgewood Industrial Park,

Uckfield, East Sussex,

TN22 5QE England

Tel: +44 (0) 1825 749494

www.naval-military-press.com

www.nmarchive.com

Contents

Document type	Place/Title	Date From	Date To
Heading	WO95/2093 (3)		
Heading	19th Division 58th Infy Bde 58th Machine Gun Coy. Mar 1916-Feb 1918		
Heading	Mar 16 To Feb 18 58 M.G. Coy Vol 1		
War Diary	Right Sector Left Division Between S.21.b.2.5 To S.10.d.1.8.	01/03/1916	07/03/1916
War Diary	Paradis.	08/03/1916	12/03/1916
War Diary	Neuve Chapelle Sector.	13/03/1916	23/03/1916
War Diary	Puresbecque	24/03/1916	25/03/1916
War Diary	Right Sector Left Division S.21.b.2.5 To S.10.d.1.8.	26/03/1916	31/03/1916
War Diary	Richebourg	01/04/1916	18/04/1916
War Diary	Robecq	19/04/1916	21/04/1916
War Diary	Erny. St. Julien	21/04/1916	06/05/1916
War Diary	Berquette.	07/05/1916	07/05/1916
War Diary	Belle Vue Farms	08/05/1916	28/05/1916
War Diary	Gorenflos	29/05/1916	29/05/1916
War Diary	Le Plessiel	30/05/1916	31/05/1916
War Diary	Erny. St. Julien	01/05/1916	06/05/1916
War Diary	Berquette.	07/05/1916	07/05/1916
War Diary	Bellevue Farm	08/05/1916	28/05/1916
War Diary	Gorenflos	29/05/1916	29/05/1916
War Diary	La Plessiel	30/05/1916	31/05/1916
War Diary	Richebourg	01/04/1916	18/04/1916
War Diary	Robecq	19/04/1916	21/04/1916
War Diary	Erny. St. Julien	22/04/1916	30/04/1916
War Diary	La Plessiel	01/06/1916	09/06/1916
War Diary	Gorenflos	10/06/1916	10/06/1916
War Diary	La Chaussee	11/06/1916	15/06/1916
War Diary	Trechencourt	16/06/1916	27/06/1916
War Diary	Bresle	28/06/1916	30/06/1916
Heading	58th Inf. Bde. 19th Div. War Diary 58th Machine Gun Company. July 1916		
War Diary	Duruacourt	01/07/1916	09/07/1916
War Diary	Baigenox	10/07/1916	20/07/1916
War Diary	Becourt Wood	21/07/1916	31/07/1916
War Diary	58th Brigade. 19th Division. 58th Brigade Machine Gun Company August 1916		
War Diary	La Houssoye	01/08/1916	03/08/1916
War Diary	Part Remy	04/08/1916	06/08/1916
War Diary	Brulooze	07/08/1916	03/09/1916
War Diary	Rabot	04/09/1916	07/09/1916
War Diary	Le Bizet	08/09/1916	20/09/1916
War Diary	Strazeele	21/09/1916	05/10/1916
War Diary	Doullens	06/10/1916	06/10/1916
War Diary	Authie	07/10/1916	07/10/1916
War Diary	Coigneux	08/10/1916	16/10/1916
War Diary	Vauchelles	17/10/1916	17/10/1916
War Diary	Herrisart	18/10/1916	18/10/1916
War Diary	Herrisart	19/10/1916	21/10/1916
War Diary	Bouzincourt	22/10/1916	30/10/1916

War Diary	Aveluy	31/10/1916	23/11/1916
War Diary	Warloy	24/11/1916	24/11/1916
War Diary	Authielle	25/11/1916	25/11/1916
War Diary	Grimont	26/11/1916	09/01/1917
War Diary	Beauval	10/01/1917	11/01/1917
War Diary	Thedell Sailly Au Bois	12/01/1917	20/02/1917
War Diary	Bus	21/02/1917	28/02/1917
War Diary	Courcelles	01/03/1917	04/03/1917
War Diary	Bus-Le-Artois	05/03/1917	09/03/1917
War Diary	Beauval	10/03/1917	11/03/1917
Miscellaneous	Occoches	12/03/1917	12/03/1917
War Diary	Sericourt	13/03/1917	13/03/1917
War Diary	Belval	14/03/1917	15/03/1917
War Diary	La. Couture	16/03/1917	17/03/1917
War Diary	Houleron	18/03/1917	18/03/1917
War Diary	Strazeele	19/03/1917	19/03/1917
War Diary	Fletre	20/03/1917	31/03/1917
War Diary	La. Clytte	01/04/1917	17/04/1917
War Diary	Curragh Camp	18/04/1917	19/04/1917
War Diary	Piebrouck.	20/04/1917	30/04/1917
War Diary	Ypres	01/05/1917	13/05/1917
War Diary	Piebrouck	14/05/1917	14/05/1917
War Diary	Wallon Capel	15/05/1917	15/05/1917
War Diary	Arques	16/05/1917	16/05/1917
War Diary	La Recousse	17/05/1917	30/05/1917
War Diary	Scherpenberg	01/06/1917	08/06/1917
War Diary	Night of	08/06/1917	20/06/1917
War Diary	S.8.b.9.7.	21/06/1917	03/07/1917
War Diary	La Polka	04/07/1917	11/07/1917
War Diary	Grand Bois.	12/07/1917	31/08/1917
War Diary	Westoutre	01/09/1917	10/09/1917
War Diary	N.10.e.5.5	11/09/1917	01/10/1917
War Diary	Shrewsbury Forest	02/10/1917	02/10/1917
War Diary	Ypres Salient	03/10/1917	31/10/1917
War Diary	Vierstraat	01/11/1917	08/11/1917
War Diary	Strazeele	09/11/1917	10/11/1917
War Diary	Ebblinghem	11/11/1917	07/12/1917
Miscellaneous	Blairville	08/12/1917	08/12/1917
War Diary	Gomie Court	09/12/1917	09/12/1917
War Diary	Etricourt	10/12/1917	11/12/1917
War Diary	Ribecourt	12/12/1917	31/12/1917
Miscellaneous	58th. Infantry Brigade	28/02/1918	28/02/1918
War Diary		01/01/1918	14/02/1918
War Diary	Le Transloy	15/02/1918	28/02/1918

19TH DIVISION
58TH INFY BDE

58TH MACHINE GUN COY.

MAR 1916 - FEB 1918

19

58 Mc Coy

Vol 1

Mar '16
to
Feb. '18

58 Company M.G.C.
March/16

Instructions regarding War Diaries and Intelligence Summaries are contained in F. S. Regs., Part II. and the Staff Manual respectively. Title Pages will be prepared in manuscript.

WAR DIARY or ~~INTELLIGENCE SUMMARY~~

(Erase heading not required.)

58 Company Machine Gun Corps

Army Form C. 2118

Place	Date	Hour	Summary of Events and Information	Remarks and references to Appendices
RIGHT SECTOR	1/3/16	6.A.M.	6 Guns in front line - 3 Guns in posts. intermittent firing - night only -	
LEFT DIVISION	2.3.16	6 A.M.	Ditto Ditto - Guns front line fired 950 rounds each Enemy Parapet -	
Between S.21.B.2.5	3 4 5	6 A.M.	Nothing to report.	
To S.10.D.1.8.	6	6 A.M.	Casualty Private Upton No. 4548 - stray bullet - Guns firing 750 rounds each -	
	7	6 A.M.	No firing allowed from Posts - no overhead fire up to date -	
	7	6 P.M.	Relief - 104th Bde taking over with Lewis Guns - War Establishment of 151 all told - leaves but 96 actual gun numbers & N.C.O.s - inadequate for 16 guns - and trench relief system - conclusion - 9 guns utmost possible to get complete relief established. -	
PARADIS.	8	6 A.M.	Rest Billets Health men - poor - reporting sick 7 per day - average - Animals - fair - with lice due quick training grooms & drivers -	
	9	6 A.M.	on 8th Parades established for Rest Billets - 7.15 A.M. Running - 9.0 Inspection Feet. 9.30 Inspection Rifles, 10 o'clock, Infantry drill, Manual Exercises, 11.0 A.M. to 1. P.M. - Section officers. -	
	10	6 A.M.	- The same -	
	11	6 A.M.	The Same, with afternoon Parade. 2 to 4 Route march under D.O. orders, to harden the men	
	12	6 A.M.	The same - Sunday.	
NEUVE CHAPELLE SECTOR.	13	10 A.M.	RELIEVED 56 Bde - 5 GUNS IN FRONT LINE - 9 IN POSTS - relieving front line by men in Posts Company in rest consist 15 available men as gunners - using 6 N.C.O.s & men per Gun in front line 4 all told in Posts - Traversing Parapet - all night - about 5000 rounds with five guns -	
	14	10 A.M.	Posts not firing yet - Building alternative night emplacements - Machine Gun Emplacements bad -	

1875 Wt. W593/826 1,000,000 4/15 J.B.C. & A. A.D.S.S./Forms/C. 2118.

58 Company M.G.C. March/16

Instructions regarding War Diaries and Intelligence Summaries are contained in F. S. Regs., Part II. and the Staff Manual respectively. Title Pages will be prepared in manuscript.

WAR DIARY

or

~~INTELLIGENCE SUMMARY~~ 58 Coy Machine Gun Corps

(Erase heading not required.)

Army Form C. 2118

Place	Date	Hour	Summary of Events and Information	Remarks and references to Appendices
NEUVE CHAPELLE SECTOR.	15	10 AM.	Night 14/15 quiet front line guns averaged 700 rounds each - wkg parties, and Parapet. —	
	16.	10 AM.	night 15/16. vertical searching LA BASSEE Road - 1000 ROUNDS.	
Do	17			
Do	18	10 AM.	Quiet. nights spent searching enemy parapet and stray working parties —	
Do	19			
	20			
Do	21.	10 AM.	Minor offensive night 20/21. by 57 Brigade. all guns active during night on enemy parapet 2000 Rounds average per gun —	
Do	22	10 AM.	Front line heavily shelled - no casualties. work started on emplacements in front line.	
Do	23	10 AM.	Relieved by 57th Brigade. marched to PURESBECQUE VIA FOSSE - LESTREM - MERVILLE. To Rest Billets.	
PURESBECQUE	24	8 pm	Day spent cleaning guns - pay of men - inspection of kit - men improving in appearance and discipline —	
Do	25	9 AM.	March to LA COUTURE - Relieving 104th Brigade in Right Sector Left Division between S.21.B.2.5 TO. S.10.D.1.8 —	
RIGHT Sector LEFT Division S.21.B.2.5 TO S.10.D.1.8.	26. 27 28 29 30 31.		Nights exceedingly quiet. much work being done on emplacements in front line for 5 guns, and keeps - 3 guns. night parties carrying timber & girders - day spent in putting them up — nothing of interest to report. —	

[illegible] Lt
for O.C. 58 Coy

Instructions regarding War Diaries and Intelligence Summaries are contained in F. S. Regs., Part II. and the Staff Manual respectively. Title Pages will be prepared in manuscript.

WAR DIARY
or
INTELLIGENCE SUMMARY
(Erase heading not required.)

Army Form C. 2118

5 8 Bde M G Coy — April 1916 — Vol 2 — 18

Place	Date	Hour	Summary of Events and Information	Remarks and references to Appendices
Richebourg	Apl 1		Night 31.3.16 - 1.4.16 Quiet - Firing at working parties - and Enemy parapet - work nearly finished No 9 Emplacement	
	2		During night nothing to report - working parties organized for carrying bricks timber etc for M.G. Emplacements	
	3		During night all quiet - all guns firing - work continued Emplacements - No 9 completed in front line	
	4		During night all quiet Factory ~~Court~~ Keep & Copse Keep Emplacements started @ 10/pm	
	5		" " " " work continued	
	6 7 8 9 10		Night quiet - work continued on Factory ~~Court~~ Keep & Copse Keep	
	11		Copse Keep completed	
	12		Factory Keep completed	
	13		Night quiet - work started on No 3 & 5 emplacements	
	14		Overhead fire - Supposed German Relief - 6 guns at 500 yds behind Front Line - situate behind Factory - Cube & Copse - fired 1500 rounds each at Cross Roads junction and communication trenches - having Enfilade effect - range 1500 to 2200 yards - Firing continued in bursts until 2.30 am. 15-4-16 Hostile reply M.G. fire & artillery - no casualties	

1875 Wt. W593/826 1,000,000 4/15 J.B.C. & A. A.D.S.S./Forms/C. 2118.

Instructions regarding War Diaries and Intelligence Summaries are contained in F. S. Regs., Part II. and the Staff Manual respectively. Title Pages will be prepared in manuscript.

No. 58 COMPANY Date April 1916 MACHINE GUN CORPS

WAR DIARY
or
INTELLIGENCE SUMMARY

(Erase heading not required.)

No. 58 COMPANY Date April 1916 MACHINE GUN CORPS

Army Form C. 2118

Place	Date	Hour	Summary of Events and Information	Remarks and references to Appendices
Richbourg	15.4.16		Factory Keep shelled - no damage - work emplacements continued. Great difficulty experienced with engineers loophole - now rectified	
	16.4.16		Night quiet - There is grave difficiency with reliefs - men having to stay in trenches 11 and 12 day to effect a relief of 4	
	17.4.16		Night quiet 105th Brigade Relieving - showed the B.M.G.O. over Line	
	18.4.16		Relief commenced 8 AM. 18.4.16 finished 3 pm. - very lengthy - order not adhered to - This tour of trenches marked by much M.G. emplacement work. carrying parties of 50 each night lent by Infantry, and 58 Coy men. Each man did at least 20 days in - and had only 8 days out - Rested in Billets night 18-19	
	19.4.16		Rested in Billets - Kit Inspection - General cleaning up -	
Robecq.	20.4.16		March 14 Miles - via Vieille Chapelle - Locon Zelobes - and high Road to Robecq. - March discipline fair.	
	21.4.16		Rested - Sorting of Limbers - under sections - indents for deficiencies	
Ecquedecques St. Julien	22.4.16		March 18 mile - Brigaded - via Lalcao Labiette Farm and High Road - Rain - March discipline excellent. men cheerful	
	23.4.16		Sunday - Holiday - men cleaning clothes etc - Voluntary Church Parades	
	24.4.16		Company training - Firing on Range at Ecquedecques St Julien - principally stoppages and action tests	

1375 Wt. W593/826 1,000,000 4/15 J.B.C. & A. A.D.S.S./Forms/C. 2118.

Instructions regarding War Diaries and Intelligence Summaries are contained in F. S. Regs., Part II. and the Staff Manual respectively. Title Pages will be prepared in manuscript.

April 1916

WAR DIARY
or
INTELLIGENCE SUMMARY
(Erase heading not required.)

April 1916

Army Form C. 2118

Place	Date	Hour	Summary of Events and Information	Remarks and references to Appendices
Erny St. Julien	24/4/16		Company training - firing on Range at Erny St Julien - principally stoppages - and action tests	
	25.4.16		Company training. Speeding up of actions - no firing	
	26.4.16		" " Tactical scheme - Intersection with Limber. speed developed coming into action	
	27.4.16		" " " " " " " at the Gallop - speed developed coming into action	
	28.4.16		Company training - Tactical scheme - Skeleton Battalion - protecting flanks - 8 guns aside - over rough ground bringing out. use of ground. masking of guns - scheme took 5 hours - ground covered about 6 miles	
	29.4.16		Company training. The same as yesterday bringing out lesson learnt previous day.	
	30.4.16		Company training. Entrenching. Quickness in digging in - using infantry trenches partly dug. South of Erny St. Julien morning only - Afternoon rest in Billets	

[signature] Capt.
COMD. No. 58 COY. MACHINE GUN CORPS.

1875 Wt. W593/826 1,000,000 4/15 J.B.C. & A. A.D.S.S./Forms/C. 2118.

Instructions regarding War Diaries and Intelligence Summaries are contained in F. S. Regs., Part II. and the Staff Manual respectively. Title Pages will be prepared in manuscript.

WAR DIARY
or
~~INTELLIGENCE~~ SUMMARY

(Erase heading not required.)

No. 58 COMPANY Date 1 May 1916 MACHINE GUN CORPS.

Army Form C. 2118

Place	Date	Hour	Summary of Events and Information	Remarks and references to Appendices
ERNY ST. JULIEN	1.5.16		Training Company - Tactical Scheme - Rearguard action -	
	2.5.16		" with Brigade - Open Fighting - Tactical scheme - man handling Guns - start to finish	
	3.5.16		" " " " " " " " " " " "	
	4.5.16		" " Division " " " " partly " " partly limbering	
	5.5.16		" " " " " " " " " " " "	
	6.5.16		Packing of Limbers cleaning of Guns, Entraining particulars	
Berguette	7.5.16		1 AM. march to Berguette - (in sections 1 section each attached to Battalions-) arrived at Berguette 7.30 A.M. Entrained 9.15 A.M. - journey took until 6.0 pm. march to Belle Vue Farm.	
Belle Vue Farm	8.5.16		Sections started arriving at Billets - 4 Hours interval between each	
	9.5.16		Rest in Billets - cleaning Guns etc	
	10.5.16		Company Training started - Limber drill practised - Route march 6 miles attached men arrived from Battalions viz. 20 9th Cheshire 20 6th Wilts. 20 9th R.W.F 20 9th Welsh. each 20 attached to nos 1. 2. 3. 4 sections respectively	
	11.5.16		Company Training - Rifle Drill - Infantry movements - Route March 8 miles Company School started - for attached men in 10 squads	
	12.5.16		Company Training Rifle Drill - Infantry movements - Route march 10 miles	
	13.5.16		Company Training - Gun Drill - School showing progress with exception of few.	
	14.5.16		" " " " etc	

1875 Wt. W593/826 1,000,000 4/15 J.B.C. & A. A.D.S.S./Forms/C. 2118.

Instructions regarding War Diaries and Intelligence Summaries are contained in F. S. Regs., Part II. and the Staff Manual respectively. Title Pages will be prepared in manuscript.

NO. 58 COMPANY Date May 1916 MACHINE GUN CORPS

WAR DIARY
or
INTELLIGENCE SUMMARY
(Erase heading not required.)

NO. 58 COMPANY Date May 1916 MACHINE GUN CORPS

Army Form C. 2118

Place	Date	Hour	Summary of Events and Information	Remarks and references to Appendices
Belle Eglise Farm	15/5/16		Company Training - Limber drill - School quite intact + a progressive training drawn up	
	16.5.16		" " Gun drill etc - Route march 10 miles	
	17.5.16		" " Limber drill - Rifle drill - Entrenching practice - Route March	
	18.5.16		" " " " " " Route March	
	19.5.16		" " " " " " " "	
	20.5.16		" " " " " " School started firing - showing good progress	
	21.5.16		Church Parade - Kit Inspection	
	22.5.16		Company Training - Running parade - Route March	
	23.5.16		" " - Afternoon Company Sports - Good Talent	
	24.5.16		Bath Parade - Company Training	
	25.5.16		Company Training - Limber drill at Gallop - Method carrying Guns	
	26.5.16		" " Infantry drill -	
	27.5.16		" " Inspection of Guns afternoon Divisional Sports	
	28.5.16		Sunday Church Parades	
Gorenflos	29.5.16		March via Flesselles - St Ouen to Gorenflos - very hot - very bad march discipline - attached men very poor - probably due to previous sedentary ten days sitting learning machine Gun	
Le Plessiel	30.5.16		March to Le Plessiel. Billeted - encouraging men to Bivouac	
	31.5.16		Rest - cleaning up - making billets inhabitable - used previously for horses cavalry	[illegible]

W. R. Biddulph
CAPT.
COMD. No. 58 COY. MACHINE GUN CORPS.

1875 Wt. W593/826 1,000,000 4/15 J.B.C. & A. A.D.S.S./Forms/C. 2118.

2nd Copy

58 M.G. Coy

Army Form C. 2118

Vols. 1. 2

XIX

APRIL & MAY

Instructions regarding War Diaries and Intelligence Summaries are contained in F. S. Regs., Part II. and the Staff Manual respectively. Title Pages will be prepared in manuscript.

WAR DIARY
or
INTELLIGENCE SUMMARY
(Erase heading not required.)

Place	Date	Hour	Summary of Events and Information	Remarks and references to Appendices
[illegible]	1.5.16		Training of Company - [illegible] - [illegible]	
	2.5.16		" [illegible] - open fighting - tactical scheme - [illegible]	
	3.5.16		" " " " " " " " " " "	
	4.5.16		" " [illegible] " " " " party " " [illegible]	
	5.5.16		" " " " " " " " " " "	
	6.5.16		Preparing to [illegible] cleaning [illegible] particulars	
[illegible]	7.5.16		[illegible] march to [illegible] (in sections 1 section each attached to Battalions) arrived at [illegible] 7.30 am [illegible] 9.15 am [illegible] marched to Belle Vue Farm	
[illegible]	8.5.16		Sections started arriving at Billets - 4 hours interval between each	
	9.5.16		Rest in Billets - cleaning Guns etc	
	10.5.16		Company training started - [illegible] practised - Route march 6 miles [illegible] from Battalions viz 20th [illegible] 20th [illegible] each [illegible] attached [illegible] sections respectively	
	11.5.16		Company training - [illegible] drill - Infantry in [illegible] - Route march [illegible] miles. Company [illegible] started [illegible] 10 squads	
	12.5.16		Company training - [illegible] - Route march 10 miles	
	13.5.16		Company training - [illegible] - [illegible] shooting practice with [illegible]	
	14.5.16		" " " " etc	

1875 Wt. W593/826 1,000,000 4/15 J.B.C. & A. A.D.S.S./Forms/C. 2118.

Instructions regarding War Diaries and Intelligence Summaries are contained in F. S. Regs., Part II. and the Staff Manual respectively. Title Pages will be prepared in manuscript.

WAR DIARY
or
INTELLIGENCE SUMMARY
(Erase heading not required.)

Army Form C. 2118

Place	Date	Hour	Summary of Events and Information	Remarks and references to Appendices
[illegible]	[illegible]/5/16		School. Company training – Limber drill – [illegible] – progressive training drawn up	
	11.5.16		" Gun drill etc – Route march 10 miles	
	13.5.16		" Limber drill – Gun drill – Entraining practice – Route march	
	15.5.16		" Route March	
	17.5.16		" "	
	20.5.16		" School closed [illegible]	
	21.5.16		Church Parade – Kit inspection	
	22.5.16		Company training – Running parade – Route march	
	23.5.16		" – [illegible] company sports – [illegible]	
	24.5.16		Route march – Company training	
	25.5.16		Company training – Limber drill at gallop – Method of [illegible]	
	26.5.16		" [illegible] drill	
	27.5.16		" Inspection & [illegible] afternoon [illegible] sports	
	28.5.16		Sunday Church Parade	
[illegible]	29.5.16		March via [illegible] – very hot – very bad march discipline – attached men very poor – probably due to previous training [illegible]	
[illegible]	30.5.16		March to [illegible] – [illegible] men to [illegible]	
	31.5.16		Rest – cleaning up – making billets habitable – and [illegible]	

1875 Wt. W593/826 1,000,000 4/15 J.B.C. & A. A.D.S.S./Forms/C. 2118.

3rd Copy

Instructions regarding War Diaries and Intelligence Summaries are contained in F. S. Regs., Part II. and the Staff Manual respectively. Title Pages will be prepared in manuscript.

~~WAR DIARY~~ or INTELLIGENCE SUMMARY

(Erase heading not required.)

Army Form C. 2118

Place	Date	Hour	Summary of Events and Information	Remarks and references to Appendices
[illegible]	1		Night 31/1 – 1-4-16 quiet – [illegible] parapet – work nearly finished No 9 emplacement	
	2		Enemy [illegible] – working parties organised for [illegible] No 4 emplacements	
	3		Enemy night all quiet – [illegible] – work continued emplacements – No 9 completed in front line	
	4		Enemy night all quiet Factory Keep [illegible] Keep [illegible]	
	5		" " " " work continued	
	6 7 8 9 10		Fairly quiet – work continued on Factory Keep and [illegible] Keep	
	11		Cabin Keep completed	
	12		Factory Keep completed	
	13		[illegible] quiet – work started on No 7 & 8 emplacement	
	14		[illegible] – [illegible] Relief – [illegible] factory – [illegible] trenches – [illegible] artillery – no casualties	

1875 Wt. W593/826 1,000,000 4/15 J.B.C. & A. A.D.S.S./Forms/C. 2118.

Instructions regarding War Diaries and Intelligence Summaries are contained in F. S. Regs., Part II. and the Staff Manual respectively. Title Pages will be prepared in manuscript.

WAR DIARY
or
INTELLIGENCE SUMMARY
(Erase heading not required.)

Army Form C. 2118

Place	Date	Hour	Summary of Events and Information	Remarks and references to Appendices
[illegible]	16.4.16		Factory Keep shelled – no damage – work improvement continued [illegible] difficulty experienced with [illegible] loophole – now [illegible]	
	17.4.16		Night quiet – [illegible] – men having to stay in trenches 11 and 12 days [illegible]	
	17.4.16		Night quiet [illegible] Brigade [illegible] – [illegible]	
	18.4.16		Relief commenced 8 am 18.4.16 [illegible] by much M.G. [illegible] by Infantry [illegible] had only 8 days out – Rested in Billets night 18-19	
	19.4.16		[illegible] – Kit Inspection – General cleaning up.	
[illegible]	20.4.16		March [illegible] Chapelle [illegible] – March [illegible] fine.	
	21.4.16		Rest [illegible] – [illegible] for [illegible]	
[illegible]	22.4.16		[illegible] High Road [illegible] discipline excellent. men cheerful	
	23.4.16		Sunday – Holiday – men cleaning clothes etc – Voluntary Church Parade	
	24.4.16		[illegible]	

1875 Wt. W593/826 1,000,000 4/15 J.B.C. & A. A.D.S.S./Forms/C. 2118.

Instructions regarding War Diaries and Intelligence Summaries are contained in F. S. Regs., Part II. and the Staff Manual respectively. Title Pages will be prepared in manuscript.

WAR DIARY
or
INTELLIGENCE SUMMARY
(Erase heading not required.)

Army Form C. 2118

Place	Date	Hour	Summary of Events and Information	Remarks and references to Appendices
[illegible]	[illegible]/16		Company Training - [illegible]	
	[illegible]		Company Training [illegible]	
	[illegible]		" " [illegible]	
	[illegible]		" " [illegible]	
	[illegible]		Company Training - [illegible] Battalion - [illegible]	
	[illegible]		Company Training. [illegible] previous day	
	[illegible]		Company Training. [illegible] in billets	

1875 Wt. W593/826 1,000,000 4/15 J.B.C. & A. A.D.S.S./Forms/C. 2118.

Instructions regarding War Diaries and Intelligence Summaries are contained in F. S. Regs., Part II. and the Staff Manual respectively. Title Pages will be prepared in manuscript.

WAR DIARY
or
INTELLIGENCE SUMMARY
(Erase heading not required.)

XIX 58 M.G. Coy

Army Form C. 2118

Vol 4 Jun

Place	Date	Hour	Summary of Events and Information	Remarks and references to Appendices
La Plessiel	1/6/16		Feet Inspection, cleaning Guns & Rifle Inspection. Sections practised in attack between trenches the following points emphasised A. actual control of individual section & guns by section & Gun Team N.C.O's. B. use of Ground C I Method of carrying ammunition etc II Communicating both laterally & to the rear by runners & visual signalling (simple Coy attack scheme) III Company practised in creeping up & running up to position under cover of our artillery fire	
	2/6/16		Training with Brigade	
	3/6/16		Feet Inspection & Rifle Inspection party of company attended Lecture (bombing) Company Drill. Gun Drill	
	4/6/16		Brigade Training.	
	5/6/16		Feet Inspection, Rifle Inspection party of company attended Lecture (bombing)	
			A I Company in attack over long distance bringing out the principle of carrying ammunition, pick shovel etc	

1875 Wt. W593/826 1,000,000 4/15 J.B.C. & A. A.D.S.S./Forms/C. 2118.

Instructions regarding War Diaries and Intelligence Summaries are contained in F. S. Regs., Part II. and the Staff Manual respectively. Title Pages will be prepared in manuscript.

WAR DIARY
or
INTELLIGENCE SUMMARY
(Erase heading not required.)

Army Form C. 2118

Place	Date	Hour	Summary of Events and Information	Remarks and references to Appendices
La Plessiel	5/6/16		I Intercommunication etc III Rapid consolidation of the captured position	
	6/6/16		Training with Brigade	
	7/6/16		Inspection, Gun Drill. Practise in rapid consolidation of the captured position	
	8/6/1916		Training with Brigade	
	9/6/16		Inspection, Gun Cleaning, unpacking & Repacking of limbers	

1875 Wt. W593/826 1,000,000 4/15 J.B.C. & A. A.D.S.S./Forms/C. 2118.

Army Form C. 2118

Instructions regarding War Diaries and Intelligence Summaries are contained in F. S. Regs., Part II. and the Staff Manual respectively. Title Pages will be prepared in manuscript.

WAR DIARY
or
INTELLIGENCE SUMMARY
(Erase heading not required.)

Place	Date	Hour	Summary of Events and Information	Remarks and references to Appendices
Gorenflos	10/6/16		March to Gorenflos.	
La Chaussee	11/6/16		March to La Chaussee	
	12/6/16		Bathing Parade, Washing Parade, Feet Inspection	
	13/6/16		Running Drill. Rifle Inspection. Unpacking & Repacking of Limber	
	14/6/16		Running Drill, Inspection, Route March Lecture to N.C.O's	
	15/6/16		Running Drill, Inspection. Route March.	
Flechencourt	16/6/16		March to Flechencourt	
	17/6/16		Gun Cleaning, Pay Parade	
	18/6/16		Church Parade,	
	19/6/16		Bath Parade, Gun Drill. Mechanism Lecture to N.C.O's	
	20/6/16		Running Drill Rifle & Equipment Inspection. Gun Cleaning Route March	
	21/6/16		Running Drill. Inspection. Gun Drill. Immediate action	
	22/6/16		Running Drill, Inftry Drill, Gun Drill. Musketry Lecture, Lecture by Capt Andrews R.A.M.C. (1st aid & use of field dressing)	

1875 Wt. W593/826 1,000,000 4/15 J.B.C. & A. A.D.S.S./Forms/C. 2118.

Army Form C. 2118

Instructions regarding War Diaries and Intelligence Summaries are contained in F. S. Regs., Part II. and the Staff Manual respectively. Title Pages will be prepared in manuscript.

WAR DIARY
or
INTELLIGENCE SUMMARY
(Erase heading not required.)

Place	Date	Hour	Summary of Events and Information	Remarks and references to Appendices
Frechencourt	23/6/16		Bathing parade, Gun drill packing of limbers Belt filling &c.	
	24/6/16		Inspection Infantry drill Belt Filling attached men on range practise	
	25/6/16		Church Parade	
	26/6/16		Feet Inspection. Belt Filling, packing of limbers &c	
	27/6/16		Overhaul of all Material. march to Bresle	
Bresle	28/6/16		Rest preparatory to going into action	
	29/6/16		General attack postponed for two days. stood fast	
	30/6/16		Church Parade. tested guns, march to Dernacourt	

[signature]
COMD. No. 59 COY MACHINE GUN CORPS

1875 Wt. W593/826 1,000,000 4/15 J.B.C. & A. A.D.S.S./Forms/C. 2118.

58th Inf.Bde.
19th Div.

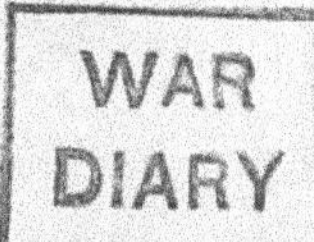

58th MACHINE GUN COMPANY.

J U L Y

1 9 1 6

Instructions regarding War Diaries and Intelligence Summaries are contained in F. S. Regs., Part II. and the Staff Manual respectively. Title Pages will be prepared in manuscript.

WAR DIARY
or
INTELLIGENCE SUMMARY
(Erase heading not required.)

Army Form C. 2118

58 MGC
Vol 5

Place	Date	Hour	Summary of Events and Information	Remarks and references to Appendices
Henencourt	1/7/16	M	March to Bellone Farm	
		[illegible]	Company left Bellone Farm for Trenches.	
	2/7/16 to 8/7/16		Company engaged in great Offensive night of the 8th company billeted in Albert.	
	9/7/16		Rest in Albert, March to Baizeux	
Baizeux	10/7/16		Unpacking of Limbers, cleaning of Guns, Repacking of Limbers.	
	11/7/16		Inspection of ammunition & Refilling of Belts &c.	
	12/7/16		Running Drill, Rifle Inspection, Bathing parade & General change of clothing	
	13/7/16		Inspection of Rifles & Equipment, refitting of clothing. Inspection by Corps Commander.	
	14/7/16		Running Drill, Rifle Inspection, Arm Drill, overhauling & repacking of limbers, Gun cleaning.	

1875 Wt. W593/826 1,000,000 4/15 J.B.C. & A. A.D.S.S./Forms/C. 2118.

Instructions regarding War Diaries and Intelligence Summaries are contained in F. S. Regs., Part II. and the Staff Manual respectively. Title Pages will be prepared in manuscript.

WAR DIARY
or
INTELLIGENCE SUMMARY
(Erase heading not required.)

Army Form C. 2118

Place	Date	Hour	Summary of Events and Information	Remarks and references to Appendices
Baizieux	15/7/16		Inspection, Infty Drill, Packing of Limbers, Inspection & Explanation of a captured German Machine Gun.	
	16/7/16		Bathing Parade, Church Parade, &c.	
	17/7/16		Running Drill, Inspection, Bett Filling, Packing of Limbers.	
	18/7/16		Inspection by Section Officers, Inspection by Brigadier General 18th Brigade	
	19/7/16		Running Drill, Infantry Drill, Gun Drill, cleaning & overhauling of guns. Examination of ammunition &c	
	20/7/16		Inspection, cleaning of Billets &c. March to Becourt Wood	
Becourt Wood	21/7/16		March from Becourt Wood to Trenches	
	25/7/16		Remained in Trenches	
	26/7/16		Relieved at 5pm and marched to Becourt Wood	
	30/7/16		March from Becourt Wood to La Houssoye 29.7.16	
	31/7/16		General Cleaning up. Bathing Parade	

J H Oliver Thompson
2/Lt 58 Coy M.G.C.

1875 Wt. W593/826 1,000,000 4/15 J.B.C. & A. A.D.S.S./Forms/C. 2118.

58th Brigade .

19th Division.

58th BRIGADE MACHINE GUN COMPANY

AUGUST 1 9 1 6::

Instructions regarding War Diaries and Intelligence Summaries are contained in F. S. Regs., Part II. and the Staff Manual respectively. Title Pages will be prepared in manuscript.

WAR DIARY
or
INTELLIGENCE SUMMARY
(Erase heading not required.)

58 M.G. Coy Vol 6

Army Form C. 2118

Place	Date	Hour	Summary of Events and Information	Remarks and references to Appendices
La Houssaye	1/8/16		Physical Training. Kit Inspection, Gun Cleaning, sorting of spare parts &c.	
	2/8/16		Physical Training, Inspection & Arm Drill, Gun Drill, Gun Cleaning. Washing of under-clothing	
	3/8/16		Cleaning Billet. March from La Houssaye to Frechencourt. Entrained at Frechencourt 11.30 am	
			Left 12 noon for Longpre Les Corps Saints arrived Longpre Les Corps Saints 3.30 p.m. Detrained & marched to Pont Remy & bivouacked.	
Pont Remy	4/8/16		Bathing parade, remainder of day (rest)	
	5/8/16		Inspection, Cleaning of Guns & accoutrements, Aquatic Sports.	
	6/8/16		March to Pont Remy Station & entrained for Bailleul, arrived 3.20 pm. Detrained & marched to Brulooze	
Brulooze	7/8/16		6 Gun Teams left for Trenches 9.30 am. day & night quiet	
	8/8/16		7 Gun Teams left for Trenches. Gun Emplacements improved & parados erected. night fairly quiet	
	9/8/16		Night quiet. Bomb store built & gun platform & emplacement improved	
	10/8/16		Night quiet. Work done Building parados & repairing Trenchboards	

Army Form C. 2118

Instructions regarding War Diaries and Intelligence Summaries are contained in F. S. Regs., Part II. and the Staff Manual respectively. Title Pages will be prepared in manuscript.

WAR DIARY
or
INTELLIGENCE SUMMARY
(Erase heading not required.)

Place	Date	Hour	Summary of Events and Information	Remarks and references to Appendices
Boulooze	11/8/16		Night quiet. Work done Screen built, & loophole of concrete emplacement made.	
	12/8/16		Night quiet, Dug out & Emplacement built	
	13/8/16		Night quiet. New loophole built, work continued on parados & parapet.	
	14/8/16		Night quiet, work done strengthening & protecting lone house to be used as M G Emplacement, also small trench dug.	
	15/8/16		Night fairly quiet, 1 Gun fired 2,000 rounds at enemy trench working party	
	16/8/16		Night quiet; concrete bottom for new emplacement laid & iron girders fixed.	
	17/8/16		Bombing attack by Enemy crushed 1 machine gun moved up to trenches as mobile reserve.	
	18/8/16		Night quiet; 3 platform built for indirect fire & dug out started	
	19/8/16		Night quiet 3 guns co-operating with artillery fired 7,000 rounds to assist in barrage put up on enemy line	

1875 Wt. W593/826 1,000,000 4/15 J.B.C. & A. A.D.S.S./Forms/C. 2118.

Army Form C. 2118

Instructions regarding War Diaries and Intelligence Summaries are contained in F. S. Regs., Part II. and the Staff Manual respectively. Title Pages will be prepared in manuscript.

WAR DIARY
or
INTELLIGENCE SUMMARY
(Erase heading not required.)

Place	Date	Hour	Summary of Events and Information	Remarks and references to Appendices
Bruloozе	20/8/16		Night quiet, platform for indirect fire built; dug out completed & open emplacement built.	
	21/8/16		Night quiet, 3 guns co-operating fired 3.000 rounds new open emplacement built.	
	22/8/16		Night quiet; platforms for indirect fire built & dug out strengthened	
	23/8/16		Night quiet. S.A.A. Store built.	
	24/8/16		Night lively, enemy bombs thrown near M. G. Emplacements, Took over old emplacements for repair	
	25/8/16		Systematic searching with 4 guns of enemy second line & supports	
	26/8/16		Same programme continued with great effect, enemy was observed running to his strong dugouts.	
	27/8/16		Night quiet. Sandbagging machine gun forw against enemy indirect ~~fire~~ Machine Gun fire.	
	28/8/16		Working parties carried on as usual building 2 open emplacements for indirect fire. Night quiet.	

1875 Wt. W593/826 1,000,000 4/15 J.B.C. & A. A.D.S.S./Forms/C. 2118.

Instructions regarding War Diaries and Intelligence Summaries are contained in F. S. Regs., Part II. and the Staff Manual respectively. Title Pages will be prepared in manuscript.

WAR DIARY
or
INTELLIGENCE SUMMARY
(Erase heading not required.)

Army Form C. 2118

Place	Date	Hour	Summary of Events and Information	Remarks and references to Appendices
Boulogne	29/8/16		Night quiet. All work at a stand-still on account of wet weather.	
	30/8/16		Working parties still unable to carry on all their work being flooded.	
	31/8/16		Unusual activity of artillery in conjunction with medium trench mortars & machine guns searched enemy's front line & supports	

J H Oliver-Thompson
2/Lt
58 Coy M G C

1875 Wt. W593/826 1,000,000 4/15 J.B.C. & A. A.D.S.S./Forms/C. 2118.

Instructions regarding War Diaries and Intelligence Summaries are contained in F. S. Regs., Part II. and the Staff Manual respectively. Title Pages will be prepared in manuscript.

WAR DIARY
or
INTELLIGENCE SUMMARY
(Erase heading not required.)

for Month September 1916

58 M G Coy

Army Form C. 2118

Vol 7

Place	Date	Hour	Summary of Events and Information	Remarks and references to Appendices
Bruloozge	1/9/16		Night Quiet Platforms built for indirect fire	
	2/9/16		Night Quiet " " " " "	
	3/9/16	M	Company relieved by 12th Canadian Brigade M.G. Coy.	
		E	Marched to Rabôt	
Rabôt	4/9/16		Cleaning of guns & sorting & cleaning of spare parts &c.	
	5/9/16		Unpacking & repacking of Limbers etc.	
	6/9/16		Lecture of Somme Tactics, Gun Drill & demonstration of overhead fire.	
	7/9/16	M	General cleaning up of Billets	
		A	Marched to Le Bizet	
Le Bizet	8/9/16		12 Teams Left for trenches & took over ~~for~~ from 68. M.G. Coy.	
	9/9/16		Night fairly quiet no work commenced	

Army Form C. 2118

Instructions regarding War Diaries and Intelligence Summaries are contained in F. S. Regs., Part II. and the Staff Manual respectively. Title Pages will be prepared in manuscript.

WAR DIARY
or
INTELLIGENCE SUMMARY
(Erase heading not required.)

Place	Date	Hour	Summary of Events and Information	Remarks and references to Appendices
Le Bizet	10/9/16		Night fairly quiet our machine guns fired at & dispersed Enemy working party.	
	11/9/16		Night quiet our machine guns fired on working party	
	12/9/16		Night quiet enemy working party dispersed	
	13/9/16		Night quiet	
	14/9/16		Night lively our machine guns fired intermittently throughout night	
	15/9/16		Night lively, our machine guns assisting in raid.	
	16/9/16		Night quiet, our machine guns fired at enemy parapet	
	17/9/16		Night quiet; our machine guns fired at enemy front line.	
	18/9/16		Night quiet.	
	19/9/16	M	Company relieved by 20th Brigade M. G. Coy. remainder of day spent in cleaning guns, unpacking & repacking of limbers	

1875 Wt. W593/826 1,000,000 4/15 J.B.C. & A. A.D.S.S./Forms/C. 2118.

Instructions regarding War Diaries and Intelligence Summaries are contained in F. S. Regs., Part II. and the Staff Manual respectively. Title pages will be prepared in manuscript.

WAR DIARY
or
INTELLIGENCE SUMMARY.
(Erase heading not required.)

Army Form C. 2118.

Hour, Date, Place	Summary of Events and Information	Remarks and references to Appendices
M. 20/9/16 La Bizet	Company marched to Strazeele, march discipline strictly maintained	
M 21/9/16 Strazeele A	Inspection, unpacking of limbers, gun cleaning, repacking of limbers.	
M 22/9/16 "	Running Drill, Inspection, Arm & Squad Drill, Gun Drill, Overhauling of spare parts	
A. "	Route March, Pay Parade	
M 23/9/16 "	Running Drill, Inspection, Arm & Squad Drill, Gun Drill, Lecture.	
A "	Route March	
24/9/16 "	Church Parades, Sports &c.	
M 25/9/16 "	Running Drill, Inspection, Gun Drill,	
A " "	Inspection by Army Commander.	
M 26/9/16 "	Running Drill, Inspection, Arm & Squad Drill, Gun Drill	
A " "	Bathing Parade	

(73989) W4141—463. 400,000. 9/14. H.&J.Ltd. Forms/C. 2118/10.

Instructions regarding War Diaries and Intelligence Summaries are contained in F. S. Regs., Part II. and the Staff Manual respectively. Title pages will be prepared in manuscript.

WAR DIARY
or
INTELLIGENCE SUMMARY.
(Erase heading not required.)

Army Form C. 2118.

Hour, Date, Place	Summary of Events and Information	Remarks and references to Appendices
M 27/9/16 Strazeele	Running Drill, Inspection Gun Drill, Arm & Squad Drill Fixing up of spare parts	
A " "	Route March	
M 28/9/16 "	Running Drill, Inspection, Arm & Squad Drill Gun Drill, Cleaning of guns	
A " "	Route March	
M 29/9/16 "	Running Drill, Inspection, Arm & Squad Drill, Sorting of & fixing up of spare parts, cleaning of guns	
A " "	Football.	
M 30/9/16 "	Running Drill, Gun Drill Arm & Squad Drill Cleaning of guns & spare parts	
A " "	Route March. Pay parade.	

J. H. Oliver Thompson
2/Lt-Adj 58 Coy. M.G.C.
for o/c.

COMD. No. 58 COY. MACHINE GUN CORPS.

(73989) W4141—463. 400,000. 9/14. H.&J.Ltd. Forms/C. 2118/10.

Instructions regarding War Diaries and Intelligence Summaries are contained in F. S. Regs., Part II. and the Staff Manual respectively. Title pages will be prepared in manuscript.

WAR DIARY
or
INTELLIGENCE SUMMARY.
(*Erase heading not required.*)

58th MG Company

for Month October 1916

Army Form C. 2118.

Vol 8

Place	Date	Hour	Summary of Events and Information	Remarks and references to Appendices
Bayeele	1/10/16	M	Church Parade	
		A	Football &c	
	2/10/16	M	Running Drill, Inspection, Arm & Squad Drill, Gun Cleaning.	
		A	Bathing Parade	
	3/10/16	M	Running Drill, Inspection, Gun Drill, Gun Cleaning	
		A	Repairing & fitting of belts.	
	4/10/16	M	Running Drill, Inspection, Gun Drill, Arm Squad Drill,	
		A	Route March.	
	5/10/16	M	General fatigues & cleaning up of billets	
		A	Company marched to BAILLEUL & entrained for DOULLENS	
Doullens	6/10/16	M	Arrived DOULLENS detrained & marched to AUTHIE Remainder of day spent in rest.	
Authie	7/10/16	M	General cleaning up of billets	
COIGNEUX		A	Marched to ROSSIGNAL FARM, COIGNEUX. 4 Teams left for trenches.	
	8/10/16	M	Church Parade	
		A	Football &c.	

2353 Wt. W2544/1454 700,000 5/15 D. D. & L. A.D.S.S. Forms/C 2118.

Instructions regarding War Diaries and Intelligence Summaries are contained in F. S. Regs., Part II. and the Staff Manual respectively. Title pages will be prepared in manuscript.

WAR DIARY
or
INTELLIGENCE SUMMARY.
(Erase heading not required.)

Army Form C. 2118.

Place	Date	Hour	Summary of Events and Information	Remarks and references to Appendices
Coigneux	9/10/16	M	Running Drill, Inspection, Infty Drill, Gun Drill.	
		A	Gun Cleaning & fixing up of spare parts. Pay Parade.	
	10/10/16	M	Running Drill, Inspection, Manouvres.	
	11/10/16	M	Running Drill, Inspection, Gun Drill, Lecture	
		A	Gun Cleaning.	
	12/10/16	M	Running Drill, Inspection. Manouvres.	
	13/10/16	M	Running Drill, Inspection, Arm & Squad Drill, Gun Drill.	
		A	Gun Cleaning.	
	14/10/16	M	Running Drill, Inspection, Fixing up of spare parts,	
		A	Gun Drill & Stoppage.	
	16/10/16	M	Church Parade.	
		A	Football &c.	
	16/10/16	M	Company relieved by 92nd Brigade M. G. Coy. Marched to VAUCHELLES & bivouacked for the night	
VAUCHELLES	17/10/16	M	Marched to HERRISART, march discipline good.	
HERRISART	18/10/16	M	General cleaning up	
		A	Pay Parade.	

2353 Wt. W2544/1454 700,000 5/15 D. D. & L. A.D.S.S. Forms/C. 2118.

Army Form C. 2118.

Instructions regarding War Diaries and Intelligence Summaries are contained in F. S. Regs., Part II. and the Staff Manual respectively. Title pages will be prepared in manuscript.

WAR DIARY
or
INTELLIGENCE SUMMARY.
(Erase heading not required.)

Place	Date	Hour	Summary of Events and Information	Remarks and references to Appendices
HERRISART	19/10/16		Inspection, unpacking & repacking of limbers.	
	20/10/16		Inspection, cleaning of guns & spare parts.	
	21/10/16		Marched to BOUZINCOURT, march discipline good.	
BOUZINCOURT	22/10/16	M	Unpacking of limbers, gun cleaning	
		A	Repacking of limbers.	
	23/10/16		Fixing up of spare parts	
	24/10/16		Belts examined & filled.	
	25/10/16		Guns thoroughly overhauled & cleaned	
	26/10/16		12 Guns went into line & relieved 56 & 57 Brigade M.G. Coys.	
	27/10/16		[illegible] lively intermittent shelling by both sides	
	28/10/16		" " " " " "	
	29/10/16		" " " " " "	
	[illegible]		[illegible] relieved by 56 & 57 Brigade M. G. Coys.	
	[illegible]		Marched to AVELUY & took over billets from 57 M. G. Coy	
AVELUY	31/10/16	M	Unpacking of limbers, gun cleaning.	
		A	Repacking of limbers.	

[illegible] T. E. [illegible] Capt

2353 Wt. W2544/1454 700,000 5/15 D. D. & L. A.D.S.S. Forms/C 2118.

Instructions regarding War Diaries and Intelligence Summaries are contained in F. S. Regs., Part II. and the Staff Manual respectively. Title pages will be prepared in manuscript.

WAR DIARY
or
INTELLIGENCE SUMMARY.

58th M.G. Coy

Army Form C. 2118.

(Erase heading not required.) for Month November 1916.

Vol 9

Place	Date	Hour	Summary of Events and Information	Remarks and references to Appendices
AVELUY	1/11/16		Cleaning of guns & spare parts.	
			Pay parade.	
	2/11/16		Company took over line from 57 Bde Machine Gun Company	
	3/11/16		Night lively, Intermittent shelling by both sides	
	4/11/16		" " " " " " "	
	5/11/16		Company relieved by 56 Bde Machine Gun Company.	
	6/11/16		Cleaning of guns & spare parts	
	7/11/16		General cleaning of equipment, rifles &c,	
			Inspection of rifles & equipment.	
	8/11/16		Inspection, cleaning & overhauling of guns.	
	9/11/16		Inspection, unpacking & repacking of limbers.	
	10/11/16		Inspection, Belt filling & examination of belt boxes	
	11/11/16		Company took over line from 57 Bde Machine Gun Company.	
	12/11/16		6 Gun Teams proceeded to line	
	13/11/16		Guns in line assisted in attack on left by overhead fire	
	14/11/16		2 Extra guns proceeded to line.	

2353 Wt. W2544/1454 700,000 5/15 D. D. & L. A.D.S.S. Forms/C. 2118.

Army Form C. 2118.

Instructions regarding War Diaries and Intelligence Summaries are contained in F. S. Regs., Part II. and the Staff Manual respectively. Title pages will be prepared in manuscript.

WAR DIARY
or
INTELLIGENCE SUMMARY.

(Erase heading not required.)

Place	Date	Hour	Summary of Events and Information	Remarks and references to Appendices
	15/11/16		Night lively, intermittent shelling by both sides.	
	16/11/16		Guns sideslipped to allow 18th Division to take over a more extended front	
	17/11/16		Hard shelling by all artillery.	
	18/11/16		4 Guns in Divisional reserve on day of attack on GRANDCOURT	
	19/11/16		Heavy shelling on newly captured ground.	
			All M. Gs. untouched.	
	20/11/16		Shelling still continued	
	21/11/16		Our Machine guns fired on enemy stragglers working parties	
	22/11/16		Company relieved by 34 Machine gun Company.	
	23/11/16		Company marched to WARLOY	
WARLOY	24/11/16		Company marched to AUTHIELLE, march discipline good	
AUTHIELLE	25/11/16		Company marched to GRIMONT	
GRIMONT	26/11/16		General cleaning up	
	27/11/16		Refitting of Clothing, Boots, &c.	
	28/11/16		Cleaning of guns & spare parts	
	29/11/16		Inspection; Arm & Squad drill, Football, &c.	

2353 Wt. W2544/1454 700,000 5/15 D. D. & L. A.D.S.S. Forms/C 2118.

Instructions regarding War Diaries and Intelligence Summaries are contained in F. S. Regs., Part II. and the Staff Manual respectively. Title pages will be prepared in manuscript.

WAR DIARY
or
INTELLIGENCE SUMMARY.
(Erase heading not required.)

Army Form C. 2118.

Place	Date	Hour	Summary of Events and Information	Remarks and references to Appendices
GRIMONT	30/11/16		Inspection, Gun Drill, Football &c.	

J.H. Ower Thompson
2/Lt [illegible] for
COMD. No. 58 COY. MACHINE GUN CORPS.

2353 Wt. W2544/1454 700,000 5/15 D. D. & L. A.D.S.S. Forms/C. 2118.

Instructions regarding War Diaries and Intelligence Summaries are contained in F. S. Regs., Part II, and the Staff Manual respectively. Title pages will be prepared in manuscript.

WAR DIARY
or
INTELLIGENCE SUMMARY.
(Erase heading not required.)

Army Form C. 2118.

58 M G Coy

for Month December 1916

Vol 10

Place	Date	Hour	Summary of Events and Information	Remarks and references to Appendices
GRIMONT	1/12/16	M	Inspection, Squad & arm Drill, Physical Training, Elementary Training.	
		A	Football	
	2/12/16	M	Running Drill, Inspection, Arm & Squad Drill, Elementary Training.	
		A	Bathing parade.	
	3/12/16	M	Church Parades	
		A	Football	
	4/12/16	M	Running Drill, Inspection, Arm & Squad Drill, Overhauling of limbers.	
		A	Football &c.	
	5/12/16	M	Running Drill, Inspection, Arm & Squad Drill, Physical Training, Bombing.	
		A	Cross Country Running.	
	6/12/16	M	Running Drill, Inspection, Arm & Squad Drill, Physical Training, Elementary Training & Bombing.	
		A	Football.	
	7/12/16	M	Running Drill, Inspection, Arm & Squad Drill, Physical Training. Elementary Training.	
		A	Football.	

2353 Wt. W2544/1454 700,000 5/15 D. D. & L. . A.D.S.S. Forms/C. 2118.

Instructions regarding War Diaries and Intelligence Summaries are contained in F. S. Regs., Part II. and the Staff Manual respectively. Title pages will be prepared in manuscript.

WAR DIARY
or
INTELLIGENCE SUMMARY.
(Erase heading not required.)

Army Form C. 2118.

Hour, Date, Place			Summary of Events and Information	Remarks and references to Appendices
GRIMONT.	8/12/16	M	Running Drill, Inspection, Arm & Squad Drill, Physical Training, Elementary Training.	
		A	Football.	
	9/12/16	M	Bathing Parade	
		A	Football & Running.	
	10/12/16	M	Church Parade	
		A	Football & Running.	
	11/12/16	M	Running Drill, Inspection, Arm & Squad Drill Physical Training, Bombing, Further Tests of Elementary Training	
		A	Football.	
	12/12/16	M	Running Drill, Inspection, Arm & Squad Drill, Physical Training & Bomb Throwing. Stoppage & cleaning of spare parts.	
		A	Football & Running.	
	13/12/16	M	Running Drill, Inspection, Squad & Arm Drill, Physical Training & Bombing. Practical Stoppage	
		A	Boxing	
	14/12/16	M	Running Drill, Inspection, Arm & Squad Drill, Physical Training, Bombing, Lecture of overhead & indirect Fire. Outdoor Scheme for Officers	
		A	Football	

(73989) W4141—463. 400,000. 9/14. H.&J.Ltd. Forms/C. 2118/10.

Instructions regarding War Diaries and Intelligence Summaries are contained in F. S. Regs., Part II. and the Staff Manual respectively. Title pages will be prepared in manuscript.

WAR DIARY
or
INTELLIGENCE SUMMARY.
(Erase heading not required.)

Army Form C. 2118.

Hour, Date, Place			Summary of Events and Information	Remarks and references to Appendices
GRIMONT	15/12/16	M	Running Drill, Inspection, Physical Training. Advanced Training & Bombing	
		A	Football, Indoor scheme for Officers	
	16/12/16	M	Bathing Parade	
		A	Football	
	17/12/16	M	Church Parade	
		A	Running & Football	
	18/12/16	M	Running Drill, Inspection, Arm & Squad Drill, Physical Training & Bombing, Mechanism	
		A	Football	
	19/12/16	M	Running Drill, Inspection, Range	
		A	Cross Country Running.	
	20/12/16	M	Running Drill, Inspection, Arm & Squad Drill, Physical Training & Bombing. Stoppages	
		A	Football.	
	21/12/16	M	Running Drill, Inspection, Arm & Squad Drill. Physical Training & Bombing, Advanced Gun Drill.	
		A	Cross Country Running & Outdoor Scheme for Officers	

(73989) W4141—463. 400,000. 9/14. H.&J.Ltd. Forms/C. 2118/10.

Instructions regarding War Diaries and Intelligence Summaries are contained in F. S. Regs., Part II. and the Staff Manual respectively. Title pages will be prepared in manuscript.

WAR DIARY
or
INTELLIGENCE SUMMARY.
(Erase heading not required.)

Army Form C. 2118.

Hour, Date, Place		Summary of Events and Information	Remarks and references to Appendices
GRIMONT 22/12/16	M	Running Drill, Inspection, Scheme of attack with M. Guns	
	A	Football & Running.	
23/12/16	M	Bathing Parade	
	A	Football	
24/12/16	M	Church Parade	
	A	Running & Football	
25/12/16	M	Church Parade	
	#		
26/12/16		Running, Boxing & Football	
27/12/16	M	Running Drill, Inspection, Arm & Squad Drill, Range	
	A	Football	
28/12/16	M	Running Drill, Inspection, Arm & Squad Drill, Physical Training, bomb throwing.	
	A	Cross Country Running.	
29/12/16	M	Running Drill, Inspection, Arm & Squad Drill, Physical Training, Gun Cleaning & belt filling	
	A	Boxing.	
30/12/16	M	Bathing Parade	J.H. Oliver-Thompson.
	A	Football	
31/12/16	M	Church Parade	Lt. & Adj. for O/C Comd. No. 52 Coy, Machine Gun Corps
	A	Football & Running.	

(73989) W4141—463. 400,000. 9/14. H.&J.Ltd. Forms/C. 2118/10.

58 Company Machine Gun Corps **WAR DIARY** for Month January 1917 Army Form C. 2118.

or

INTELLIGENCE SUMMARY.

(Erase heading not required.)

Instructions regarding War Diaries and Intelligence Summaries are contained in F. S. Regs., Part II. and the Staff Manual respectively. Title pages will be prepared in manuscript.

Vol XI

Place	Date	Hour	Summary of Events and Information	Remarks and references to Appendices
GRIMONT	1/1/17	M	Running Drill, Inspection	
		A	Football & Boxing	
	2/1/17	M	Running Drill, Inspection, Arm & Squad Drill, Physical Training Stoppages	
		A	Cross Country Running	
	3/1/17	M	Running Drill, Inspection, Arm & Squad Drill, Physical Training Practical Stoppage	
		A	Football	
	4/1/17	M	Running Drill, Inspection, Arm & Squad Drill, Physical Training Gun Cleaning	
		A	Football	
	5/1/17	M	Running Drill, Range	
		A	Gun Cleaning	
	6/1/17	M	Bathing Parade	
		A	Boxing	
	7/1/17	M	Church Parade	
		A	Boxing	
	8/1/17	M	Running Drill, Inspection, Arm & Squad Drill, Physical Training Gun Cleaning	
		A	Packing of Limbers.	

A5834 Wt. W4973/M687 750,000 8/16 D. D. & L. Ltd. Forms/C.2118/13.

Instructions regarding War Diaries and Intelligence Summaries are contained in F. S. Regs., Part II. and the Staff Manual respectively. Title pages will be prepared in manuscript.

WAR DIARY
or
INTELLIGENCE SUMMARY.
(Erase heading not required.)

Army Form C. 2118.

Place	Date	Hour	Summary of Events and Information	Remarks and references to Appendices
GRIMONT	9/1/17	M	Company left & marched to BEAUVAL	
BEAUVAL	10/1/17	M	Inspection, unpacking of limbers, gun cleaning	
		A	Repacking of limbers	
	11/1/17	M	Company left in motor lorries for ~~the~~ THE DELL SAILLY au BOIS	
		A	8 Teams went into Trenches & took over from 94th Brigade.	
THE DELL SAILLY au BOIS	12/1/17		Repairs to Billet commenced	
			Occasional shelling on both sides. FAITH ST position blown up.	
	13/1/17	M	Brigadier General inspected billets.	
			New Emplacement for BATEUSE commenced.	
			FAITH ST position again heavily shelled.	
	14/1/17	M	Bathing parade for sections in reserve.	
		A	work on billets & Transport lines continued	
	15/1/17	M	Brigadier General Inspection Gun Positions	
			Night comparatively quiet. No 1 & 4 Section relieved by 2 & 3 Sections	
	16/1/17	"	Very little enemy activity, work on emplacement proceeded with.	
	17/1/17		Night quiet, work on emplacement still carried on	
	18/1/17		The sector embracing PELLISIER, REVEL, BATEUSE, & FAITH. ST taken over by 57th Brigade	
			6 Teams relieved the 96th Brigade in a new sector on the right.	

A5834 Wt. W4973/M687 750,000 8/16 D. D. & L. Ltd. Forms/C.2118/13.

Instructions regarding War Diaries and Intelligence Summaries are contained in F. S. Regs., Part II. and the Staff Manual respectively. Title pages will be prepared in manuscript.

Army Form C. 2118.

WAR DIARY
or
INTELLIGENCE SUMMARY.
(Erase heading not required.)

Place	Date	Hour	Summary of Events and Information	Remarks and references to Appendices
THE DELL SAILLY AU BOIS	19/1/17		Night quiet, work on emplacement carried on.	
	20/1/17		4 Teams relieved the teams holding the following gun positions CAVONTY, CEMETERY, FORT MARIE LOUISE, BRISOUX.	
	21/1/17		Night quiet, keen frost & snow. emplacement completed.	
	22/1/17		6 Teams + 2 Officers relieved Teams on right sector. normal activity on both sides.	
	23/1/17		Bunking of billets continued. Night quiet. Increased activity of enemy aeroplanes. Gun in front line opened fire on enemy aeroplane flying low.	
	24/1/17		4 Teams relieved on left sector. Increased enemy artillery activity. weather bright & frosty.	
	25/1/17		Night quiet, HEBUTERNE intermittently shelled with gas shells. Enemy appears to be registering his own front line. Part of company paid.	
	26/1/17		6 Teams + 2 Officers relieved on right sector. Situation normal. Brigadier General inspected gun positions in line.	
	27/1/17		Night quiet. Enemy aeroplane active behind our lines. open emplacement in left subsector complete. Part of company paid.	
	28/1/17		A screen & other arrangements for overhead fire completed.	
	29/1/17		Night quiet.	

A3834 Wt. W4973/M687 · 750,000 8/16 D. D. & L. Ltd. Forms/C.2118/13

Army Form C. 2118.

Instructions regarding War Diaries and Intelligence Summaries are contained in F. S. Regs., Part II. and the Staff Manual respectively. Title pages will be prepared in manuscript.

WAR DIARY
or
INTELLIGENCE SUMMARY.

(Erase heading not required.)

Place	Date	Hour	Summary of Events and Information	Remarks and references to Appendices
THE DELL SAILLY AU BOIS	30/1/17		6 Teams relieved on the right subsector night comparatively quiet	
	31/1/17		Night & day quiet	

R.A. Cox, Major
COMD. No. 55 COY. MACHINE GUN CORPS.

A5834 Wt. W4973/M687 750,000 8/16 D. D. & L. Ltd. Forms/C.2118/13.

Instructions regarding War Diaries and Intelligence Summaries are contained in F. S. Regs., Part II. and the Staff Manual respectively. Title pages will be prepared in manuscript.

WAR DIARY or INTELLIGENCE SUMMARY.

(Erase heading not required.)

58 Company M. G. Corps.

Army Form C. 2118.

Vol 12

Place	Date	Hour	Summary of Events and Information	Remarks and references to Appendices
THE DELL SAILLY au BOIS	1/2/17		Night quiet. Teams relieved on left subsector	
	2/2/17		Night quiet. New night firing emplacement built.	
	3/2/17		Considerable artillery activity	
	4/2/17		Night quiet.	
	5/2/17		Teams relieved on left subsector	
	6/2/17		Heavy shelling on both sides	
	7/2/17		Continued heavy shelling. Aeroplanes very active.	
	8/2/17		Night emplacements constructed at K 22 B. 3. 4.	
	9/2/17		Teams on left subsector relieved.	
	10/2/17		Additional Team proceeded to line to take over new emplacement	
	11/2/17		Day & Night quiet.	
	12/2/17		Our front line trenches heavily bombarded in early morning	
	13/2/17		Anti-aircraft Machine Gun mounted in CEMETERY. Teams relieved on left subsector	
	14/2/17		Day & night quiet.	

A5834 Wt. W4973/M687 750,000 8/16 D. D. & L. Ltd. Forms/C.2118/13.

Instructions regarding War Diaries and Intelligence Summaries are contained in F. S. Regs., Part II. and the Staff Manual respectively. Title pages will be prepared in manuscript.

WAR DIARY
or
INTELLIGENCE SUMMARY.
(Erase heading not required.)

Army Form C. 2118.

Place	Date	Hour	Summary of Events and Information	Remarks and references to Appendices
THE DELL SAILLY AU BOIS	15/2/17		Anti aircraft Machine Gun took up position in BLUE LINE to deal with hostile planes hovering over battery positions.	
	16/2/17		HEBUTERNE & vicinity of SAILLY shelled by 5.9 Howitzer.	
	17/2/17		2 Teams with anti aircraft Machine guns took position near COIGNEUX shell dump.	
			5 Extra Teams proceeded into line on right subsector.	
	18/2/17		Back areas of Brigade & front line system subject to heavy bombardment.	
			2 Anti-aircraft gun Teams at COIGNEUX relieved.	
	19/2/17		Retaliation for bombardment of back areas	
	20/2/17		Company relieved by the 92nd Brigade Machine Gun Coy.	
			Left Billets at THE DELL & marched to BUS	
BUS	21/2/17		Cleaning of Guns, spare parts &c.	
	22/2/17		General cleaning up of equipment, rifles, and repairing of billets.	
	23/2/17		Inspection, Mechanism.	
	24/2/17		Inspection, Stoppage. Gas Helmet Drill	

2353 Wt. W2544/1454 700,000 5/15 D. D. & L. A.D.S.S./Forms/C. 2118.

Instructions regarding War Diaries and Intelligence Summaries are contained in F. S. Regs., Part II. and the Staff Manual respectively. Title pages will be prepared in manuscript.

WAR DIARY
or
INTELLIGENCE SUMMARY.
(Erase heading not required.)

Army Form C. 2118.

Place	Date	Hour	Summary of Events and Information	Remarks and references to Appendices
BUS	25/2/17		Church Parade. Football.	
	26/2/17		Inspection, Gun cleaning [illegible] up of spare parts.	
			Belt filling & Belt clea[illegible]	
	27/2/17		Brigade Training.	
	28/2/17		Coy left billets at BUS & proceeded to line	
			4 guns placed in posts	
				[illegible] Thompson Lt.

2353 Wt. W2544/1454 700,000 5/15 D. D. & L. A.D.S.S. Forms/C. 2118.

Vol 13

Army Form C. 2118.

Instructions regarding War Diaries and Intelligence Summaries are contained in F. S. Regs., Part II. and the Staff Manual respectively. Title pages will be prepared in manuscript.

WAR DIARY
or
INTELLIGENCE SUMMARY.
(Erase heading not required.)

58 Company. M.G. Corps.
for month of March 1917

Place	Date	Hour	Summary of Events and Information	Remarks and references to Appendices
COURCELLES	1/3/17		4 posts held by 57 Brigade M.G. Coy relieved by our guns	
	2/3/17		4 more guns took part in the attack.	
	3/3/17		Company relieved by the 92nd Brigade M.G. Coy.	
	4/3/17		Company left billets at COURCELLES & took over billets at BUS-les-ARTOIS	
BUS-le-ARTOIS	5/3/17	M	General cleaning up of equipment & arms.	
		A	Cleaning of guns & spare parts.	
	6/3/17	M	Inspection, Infantry Drill, Gun Drill, Stoppage.	
		A	Recreational Training	
	7/3/17		50 men on fatigue (working party at railhead) remainder of company bathing parade.	
	8/3/17		Half of company bathing parade Remainder of company route march.	
	9/3/17		Route march.	
BEAUVAL	10/3/17		Company marched to BEAUVAL march discipline good.	
	11/3/17		Company marched to OCCOCHES march discipline good.	

A5834 Wt. W4973/M687 750,000 8/16 D. D. & L. Ltd. Forms/C.2118/13.

Instructions regarding War Diaries and Intelligence Summaries are contained in F. S. Regs., Part II. and the Staff Manual respectively. Title pages will be prepared in manuscript.

WAR DIARY
or
INTELLIGENCE SUMMARY.
(Erase heading not required.)

Army Form C. 2118.

Place	Date	Hour	Summary of Events and Information	Remarks and references to Appendices
OCCOCHES	12/3/17		Cleaning of Equipment & arms remainder of day spent in rest.	
SERICOURT	13/3/17		Company marched to SERICOURT march discipline good	
BELVAL	14/3/17		Company march to BELVAL march discipline good	
	15/3/17		Cleaning of Equipment & arms remainder of day spent in rest.	
LA.COUTURE	16/3/17		Company marched to LA.COUTURE march discipline good	
	17/3/17		Cleaning of equipment & arms remainder of day spent in rest.	
HOULERON	18/3/17		Company marched to HOULERON march discipline good	
STRAZEELE	19/3/17		Company marched to STRAZEELE march discipline good	
FLETRE	20/3/17		Company marched to FLETRE marched discipline good	
	21/3/17	M	Inspection, Infantry Drill, Gun Cleaning	
		A	Pay Parade	
	22/3/17	M	Inspection, Infantry Drill, Stoppages, Gun Drill	
		A	Recreational Training.	

A5834 Wt. W4973/M687 750,000 8/16 D. D. & L. Ltd. Forms/C.2118/13.

Instructions regarding War Diaries and Intelligence Summaries are contained in F. S. Regs., Part II. and the Staff Manual respectively. Title pages will be prepared in manuscript.

WAR DIARY
or
INTELLIGENCE SUMMARY.
(Erase heading not required.)

Army Form C. 2118.

Place	Date	Hour	Summary of Events and Information	Remarks and references to Appendices
FLETRE	23/3/17	M	Inspection, Infantry drill, Stoppage, overhauling of guns	
		A	Washing limbers	
	24/3/17	M	Inspection, Infantry drill, Stoppage, overhauling of spare parts	
		A	Recreational Training.	
	25/3/17		Church Parade.	
	26/3/17	M	Inspection, Infantry Drill, Saluting Drill,	
		A	Inspection by Corps Commander.	
	27/3/17	M	Inspection, Infantry Drill, Saluting drill, Mechanism, Stoppage	
		A	Part of company inoculated.	
	28/3/17	M	Inspection, Saluting drill, Gun drill,	
		A	Recreational Training.	
	29/3/17	M	Inspection, Infantry drill, Saluting drill, Gun Drill,	
		A	Recreational Training.	
	30/3/17	M	Half of Company proceeded to relieve half of 57 Brigade M.G. Coy at LA CLYTTE	
	31/3/17	M	Remainder of Company proceeded to LA CLYTTE 8 Guns proceeded into line.	

for J.H. [illegible] Thompson

A5834 Wt. W4973/M687 750,000 8/16 D. D. & L. Ltd. Forms/C.2118/13.

Instructions regarding War Diaries and Intelligence Summaries are contained in F. S. Regs., Part II. and the Staff Manual respectively. Title pages will be prepared in manuscript.

WAR DIARY
or
INTELLIGENCE SUMMARY.
(Erase heading not required.)

Army Form C. 2118.

58 Cav. M. G. Corps.

For April 1917

14

Hour, Date, Place		Summary of Events and Information	Remarks and references to Appendices
LA-CLYTTE	1.4.1917	Night fairly quiet.	
	2.4.1917	Slight activity of artillery by both sides.	
	3.4.1917	Night quiet.	
	4.4.1917	Artillery active. Gun Teams relieved.	
	5.4.1917	Our artillery heavily bombarded enemy's front line & support line in GRAND-BOIS.	
	6.4.1917	Enemy Trench Mortar active on our front line during action on right. Enemy blew up small mine to our right in NO MANS LAND	
	7.4.1917	Artillery active on both sides.	
	8.4.1917	Night fairly quiet. Gun Teams relieved.	
	9.4.1917	Activity of enemy artillery on back areas	
	10.4.1917	Night fairly quiet	
	11.4.1917	Artillery active on GRAND-BOIS	
	12.4.1917	Night quiet, Gun Teams relieved,	
	13.4.1917	Enemy artillery active on RIDGE WOOD. Enemy aircraft active	
	14.4.1917	Artillery active ~~on~~ both sides. Enemy's Trench Mortar active at various intervals	

(73989) W4141—463. 400,000. 9/14. H.&J.Ltd. Forms/C. 2118/10.

Instructions regarding War Diaries and Intelligence Summaries are contained in F. S. Regs., Part II. and the Staff Manual respectively. Title pages will be prepared in manuscript.

WAR DIARY
or
INTELLIGENCE SUMMARY.
(Erase heading not required.)

Army Form C. 2118.

Place	Hour, Date, Place		Summary of Events and Information	Remarks and references to Appendices
LA CLYTTE	15. 4. 1917		Artillery, Trench Mortar, & machine guns active on both sides.	
	16. 4. 1917		Night fairly quiet. Our aeroplanes very active.	
	17. 4. 1917		Company relieved by 56th Bde. M. G. Coy.	
			Company took over billet of 17 M. G. Coy at CURRAGH CAMP	
CURRAGH CAMP	18. 4. 1917	M	Cleaning of guns & spare parts	
		A	Overhauling of limbers.	
	19. 4. 1917		Company marched to PIEBROUCK	
PIEBROUCK	20. 4. 1917	M	Running Drill, Inspection, Infantry Drill, Stoppage, Gun Drill	
		A	Football.	
	21. 4. 1917	M	Running Drill, Inspection, Infantry Drill, Stoppage.	
		A	Route March.	
	22. 4. 1917	M	Church Parades	
		A	Football	
	23. 4. 1917	M	Running Drill, Inspection, Infantry Drill, Physical Training	
			Demonstration of Indirect Fire	
		A	Football	
	24. 4. 1917	M	Running Drill, Inspection, Infantry Drill, Stoppage.	
			Physical Training, Advanced Gun Drill	
		A	Cross Country Run.	

(73989) W4141—463. 400,000. 9/14. H.&J.Ltd. Forms/C. 2118/10.

Instructions regarding War Diaries and Intelligence Summaries are contained in F. S. Regs., Part II. and the Staff Manual respectively. Title pages will be prepared in manuscript.

WAR DIARY
or
INTELLIGENCE SUMMARY.
(Erase heading not required.)

Army Form C. 2118.

Hour, Date, Place			Summary of Events and Information	Remarks and references to Appendices
PIEBROUCK	25.4.17	M	Running Drill, Inspection, Infantry drill, Stoppages. Physical Training, cleaning & repacking of limbers	
		A	Football.	
	26.4.17	M	Brigade Training.	
	27.4.17	M	Range practice	
		A	Cleaning of guns	
	28.4.17	M	Running Drill, Inspection, Infantry drill, Stoppages. Physical Training, Belt Filling. Map reading.	
		A	Football. Pay Parade.	
	29.4.17		Company marched to RENINGHELST.	
	30.4.17		Company marched to YPRES. 16 guns Teams proceeded into line & took over from 68 M.G. Coy.	

J.H. Dove Thompson Lt
for Comd. No. 62 Coy. Machine Gun Corps.

(73989) W4141—463. 400,000. 9/14. H.&J.Ltd. Forms/C. 2118/10.

Instructions regarding War Diaries and Intelligence Summaries are contained in F. S. Regs., Part II. and the Staff Manual respectively. Title pages will be prepared in manuscript.

WAR DIARY or INTELLIGENCE SUMMARY.

(Erase heading not required.)

58 Company, M. G. Corps — Army Form C. 2118.

for Month May 1917

Vol 15

Place	Date	Hour	Summary of Events and Information	Remarks and references to Appendices
YPRES	1/5/17		Slight artillery activity on both side. Great aerial activity by both side	
	2/5/17		Enemy artillery very active on back areas own artillery shelled SANCTUARY WOOD	
	3/5/17		Enemy artillery shelled back areas Slight aerial activity	
	4/5/17		Enemy artillery fairly active. Hostile aircraft very active during day Our A.A. Guns fired at enemy aeroplane and it was observed to descend as if hit by our A.A. Guns.	
	5/5/17		Enemy artillery heavily shelled back areas.	
	6/5/17		Enemy artillery heavily shelled YPRES, also ZILLEBEKE & DORMY areas Enemy aeroplane brought down in the vicinity of ZILLEBEKE	
	7/5/17		Artillery very active on both side Machine Gun fired 250 rounds at enemy aircraft	
	8/5/17		Enemy artillery shelled ZILLEBEKE & DORMY HOUSE 3 mines went up on our right.	
	9/5/17		Enemy artillery fairly active during day. Violent bombardment at night Enemy aircraft very active during day.	
	10/5/17		Intense bombardment by both side. Enemy made a raid between the hours of 3.20 AM & 4.20 AM. Enemy aircraft very active.	
	11/5/17		Enemy artillery shelled intermittently throughout the day in the neighbourhood of SANCTUARY WOOD Our Machine Gun fired 300 rounds at Enemy aircraft between the hours 8pm & 9pm	

A5834 Wt. W4973/M687 750,000 8/16 D. D. & L. Ltd. Forms/C.2118/13.

Instructions regarding War Diaries and Intelligence Summaries are contained in F. S. Regs., Part II. and the Staff Manual respectively. Title pages will be prepared in manuscript.

WAR DIARY
or
INTELLIGENCE SUMMARY.
(*Erase heading not required.*)

Army Form C. 2118.

Place	Date	Hour	Summary of Events and Information	Remarks and references to Appendices
YPRES	12/5/17	M	Enemy shelled back areas	
		E	Company relieved by 70th Brigade M G Company	
	13/5/17	M	Company marched to WINNEPEG CAMP remainder of morning company rested.	
		E	Company left & marched to PIEBROUCK.	
PIEBROUCK	14/5/17	M	Cleaning of guns & repacking of limbers	
		A	Pay of Company	
WALLON CAPEL	15/5/17	M	Company left & marched to WALLON CAPPEL	
ARQUES	16/5/17	M	Company left & marched to ARQUES	
LA RECOUSSE	17/5/17	M	Company left & marched to LA RECOUSSE march discipline strictly maintained.	
	18/5/17	M	Inspection, Infty Drill, Immediate action. Immediate action Lecture & Demonstration of Machine Gun Barrage Fire.	
		A	Recreational Training	
	19/5/17	M	Running Drill, Inspection, Infantry Drill, Stoppage. Carrying Gun Tripod & Ammunition specified distance.	
		A	Football	
	20/5/17	M	Running Drill, Inspection, Infty Drill, Stoppage, Gun Drill. Carrying Gun, Tripod, & ammunition specified distances	
	21/5/17		Brigade Training	

A5834 Wt. W4973/M687 750,000 8/16 D. D. & L. Ltd. Forms/C.2118/13.

Instructions regarding War Diaries and Intelligence Summaries are contained in F. S. Regs., Part II. and the Staff Manual respectively. Title pages will be prepared in manuscript.

WAR DIARY
or
INTELLIGENCE SUMMARY.
(Erase heading not required.)

Army Form C. 2118.

Place	Date	Hour	Summary of Events and Information	Remarks and references to Appendices
	22/5/17	M	Running Drill, Inspection, Infantry Drill, Stoppage Gun Drill Carrying Gun Tripod & ammunition specified distance	
		A	Football	
	23/5/17		Brigade Training	
	24/5/17	M	Inspection. Route march.	
		A	Football.	
	25/5/17	M	Company marched to WATTEN and entrained for BAILLEUL	
		A	Company detrained at BAILLEUL & marched to SCHERPENBERG CAMP	
	26/5/17	M	Inspection Infantry drill, Cleaning of Guns	
		A	General fatigues, Pay parade.	
	27/5/17	M	Inspection, Inftry drill, Repacking of limber	
		A	Cleaning of Belts & Belt filling	
	28/5/17	M	Inspection, Inftry drill, lecture & demonstration on the YUKON PACK	
		A	Fixing up of spare parts	
	29/5/17	M	Inspection, Inftry Drill, Bathing parade	
		A	5 Gun Teams proceeded into line & took over from 57th M.G. Coy.	
	30/5/17		8 guns emplacements being prepared. Artillery very active on both sides, also our own machine guns. Work on gun emplacements still carried on	
	31/5/17		Artillery quiet on both sides during the day work on gun emplacements continued.	

for John Kinsella 2/Lt
COMD. No. 56 [illegible] MACHINE GUN CORPS

A5834 Wt. W4973/M687 750,000 8/16 D. D. & L. Ltd. Forms/C.2118/13.

Instructions regarding War Diaries and Intelligence Summaries are contained in F. S. Regs., Part II. and the Staff Manual respectively. Title pages will be prepared in manuscript.

WAR DIARY
or
INTELLIGENCE SUMMARY.
(*Erase heading not required.*)

58 Company. M. G. Corps
for June 1917.

Army Form C. 2118.

Vol 16

Hour, Date, Place		Summary of Events and Information	Remarks and references to Appendices
SCHERPENBERG	1/6/17	Artillery very active on both sides.	
	2/6/17	Artillery very active on both sides. Enemy Trench Mortars active on our front line.	
	3/6/17	Artillery very active on both sides.	
	4/6/17	Enemy heavily shelled our old & new reserve line.	
	5/6/17	Artillery very active on both sides.	
	6/6/17	Artillery very active on both sides.	
	7/6/17	The Company engaged in the Offensive to the north of WYTSCHAETE. All objectives gained & new line consolidated. 8 Guns attacked with the Brigade. 8 Guns opened Barrage fire in conjunction with the artillery & on completion followed up the attacking troops & helped in the consolidation.	
	8/6/17	Consolidating & holding new line East of OOSTTAVERNE	
night of	19-20/6/17	Company marched to S.8.b.9.7. Sheet 28.S.W	
S.8.b.9.7.	21/6/17 M A	Inspections, cleaning & packing of limbers. Pay parade.	

W Eastwaite
Capt
O.C. No. 58 Coy. Machine Gun

(73989) W4141—463. 400,000. 9/14. H.&J.Ltd. Forms/C. 2118/10.

Instructions regarding War Diaries and Intelligence Summaries are contained in F. S. Regs., Part II. and the Staff Manual respectively. Title pages will be prepared in manuscript.

WAR DIARY
or
INTELLIGENCE SUMMARY.

(Erase heading not required.)

Army Form C. 2118.

Hour, Date, Place		Summary of Events and Information	Remarks and references to Appendices
S.8.b.9.7	22/6/17	Company Inspected by G.O.C., 58 Brigade.	
	23/6/17 M	Inspection, Infantry Drill, Stoppage, Gun cleaning.	
	A	Recreational Training.	
	24/6/17	Church Parade.	
	25/6/17 M	Running Drill, Inspection, Infantry Drill, Stoppage, Physical Training, Gun Drill.	
	A	Recreational Training	
	26/6/17 M	Running Drill, Inspection, Infantry Drill, Gun Drill, Physical Training Practice in barrage fire & technical M.G. Instruction	
	A	Recreational Training.	
	27/6/17 M	Running Drill, Range.	
	A	Pay Parade	
	28/6/17 M	Running Drill, Range.	
	A	Brigade Sports.	
	29/6/17 M	Running Drill, Inspection, Infantry Drill, Physical Training Mechanism, Stoppage	
	A	Company Inspected by G.O.C., Division.	
	30/6/17 M	Running Drill, Inspection, Gun Drill, Belt Filling.	
	A	Recreational Training.	

W. [illegible]thwaite Lt.

(73989) W4141—463. 400,000. 9/14. H.&J.Ltd. Forms/C. 2118/10.

58 Coy. M. G. Corps

Instructions regarding War Diaries and Intelligence Summaries are contained in F. S. Regs., Part II. and the Staff Manual respectively. Title pages will be prepared in manuscript.

WAR DIARY

or

~~INTELLIGENCE SUMMARY~~. for month July 1917

(*Erase heading not required.*)

Army Form C. 2118.

Vol 17

	Hour, Date, Place		Summary of Events and Information	Remarks and references to Appendices
S.8.b.9.7	1/7/17		Church Parade	
	2/7/17	M	Inspection, Infantry Drill, Physical Training, Gun Cleaning	
		A	Repacking of limbers	
	3/7/17	M	Company left & marched to LA.POLKA N.31.d.6.6.	
LA:POLKA	4/7/17	M	Inspection, Infantry Drill, Instruction in use of M. Gun in defence against enemy aircraft	
		A	practical demonstration in indirect fire. use of clinometer & direction explained.	
	5/7/17	M	Running Drill, Inspection, Infty Drill, Physical Training Indirect fire & use of depression stop. practice in the use of German Machine Gun.	
		A	Combined drill & signal. Sight setting & laying	
	6/7/17	M	Inspection, Infty Drill, Physical Training, Signal Training	
		A	Gun Cleaning.	
	7/7/17	M	Inspection Infty Drill Physical Training. Bath parade	
		A	Advanced drill for M. G.	
	8/7/17		Church Parade.	
	9/7/17	M	Inspection, Infantry Drill, cleaning & overhauling of Guns & Spare parts.	
		A	Lecture & Demonstration in anti aircraft Tactics.	
	10/7/17		Inspection, Infty Drill Stripping & cleaning of guns fixing up of spare parts	

(73989) W4141—463. 400,000. 9/14. H.&J.Ltd. Forms/C. 2118/10.

Army Form C. 2118

WAR DIARY

~~INTELLIGENCE SUMMARY~~

(Erase heading not required.)

Instructions regarding War Diaries and Intelligence Summaries are contained in F. S. Regs., Part II. and the Staff Manual respectively. Title Pages will be prepared in manuscript.

Place	Date	Hour	Summary of Events and Information	Remarks and references to Appendices
LA POLKA	11/7/17	M	Overhauling of Belt boxes & ammunition	
		E	Company left & took over line from 57th M. G. Coy.	
GRAND BOIS.	12/7/17		Artillery activity by both sides.	
			Our Machine guns active against enemy aircraft, one enemy aircraft driven down in our lines.	
	13/7/17		Enemy artillery active at intervals during day, increased activity by night.	
			alternative emplacement for guns constructed at PRESTON DUMP.	
			Emplacement for guns at OOSTAVERNE WOOD completed & sandbagged.	
	14/7/17		Enemy artillery intermittent throughout the day on our front line.	
			our artillery fairly active " " "	
			our Machine guns active during night.	
	15/7/17		Enemy Artillery quiet during day, fairly active at night.	
			Aircraft activity by both sides.	
	16/7/17		Enemy artillery active on OOSTAVERNE WOOD.	
			aircraft very active by both sides, 1 Enemy aircraft driven down in own lines & 1 destroyed.	
	17/7/17		Enemy Artillery & Machine Guns fairly active.	
			our artillery very active day & night.	
	18/7/17		Enemy heavily shelled our front line. Enemy aircraft very active.	
			our Machine Guns assisted in raid on JUNCTION BUILDINGS.	
	19/7/17		Artillery activity by both sides. Aircraft activity by both sides.	

1875 Wt. W593/826 1,000,000 4/15 J.B.C. & A. A.D.S.S./Forms/C. 2118.

Instructions regarding War Diaries and Intelligence Summaries are contained in F. S. Regs., Part II. and the Staff Manual respectively. Title Pages will be prepared in manuscript.

WAR DIARY

Army Form C. 2118

(Erase heading not required.)

Place	Date	Hour	Summary of Events and Information	Remarks and references to Appendices
GRAND BOIS.	20/7/17		Artillery activity by both side.	
	21/7/17		Enemy artillery quiet during day. Enemy heavily shelled our front line throughout the night. Increase of enemy kite balloons.	
	22/7/17		Enemy artillery & Machine Guns fairly active. our Machine Guns assisted in raid on JUNCTION BUILDINGS.	
	23/7/17		Enemy artillery active at intervals. Enemy M. Guns active on OOSTAVERNE X ROADS.	
	24/7/17		Artillery activity by both sides. Enemy machine guns active. aircraft activity by both sides.	
	25/7/17		Artillery activity by both side. Enemy machine guns active at intervals during night. Slight enemy aircraft activity.	
	26/7/17		Artillery activity by both side. Slight aircraft activity during the hours of 4 pm & 8 pm. Enemy M. G's fired intermittently throughout the night. Work commenced on 16 new gun emplacements.	
	27/7/17		Enemy artillery quiet during day probably owing to visibility. Very active during night. 16 Gun Emplacements completed.	
	28/7/17		Artillery activity during day by both side. Enemy aircraft quiet during day, 2 planes appeared over our line about 10.30 pm. Our aircraft very active.	
	29/7/17		Enemy M Guns active at sign of any movement near our front line. Enemy snipers active. artillery fairly quiet on both side.	

1875 Wt. W593/826 1,000,000 4/15 J.B.C. & A. A.D.S.S./Forms/C. 2118.

Army Form C. 2118

Instructions regarding War Diaries and Intelligence Summaries are contained in F. S. Regs., Part II. and the Staff Manual respectively. Title Pages will be prepared in manuscript.

WAR DIARY

(Erase heading not required.)

Place	Date	Hour	Summary of Events and Information	Remarks and references to Appendices
	30/7/17		Guns moved to Barrage positions in anticipation of an Offensive	
	31/7/17		Guns fired Barrage in cooperation with Artillery for the Offensive	

[illegible signature]

for COMD. No. 58 COY. MACHINE GUN CORPS.

1875 Wt. W593/826 1,000,000 4/15 J.B.C. & A. A.D.S.S./Forms/C. 2118.

Instructions regarding War Diaries and Intelligence Summaries are contained in F. S. Regs., Part II. and the Staff Manual respectively. Title pages will be prepared in manuscript.

WAR DIARY
or
INTELLIGENCE SUMMARY.
(Erase heading not required.)

58 M.G. Coy

for month of August 1917

Vol 18

Army Form C. 2118.

Place	Date	Hour	Summary of Events and Information	Remarks and references to Appendices
	1/8/17		Company with 16 Guns in the line in barrage positions in groups. Each group fired one gun continuously throughout the day and night. Offensive successful except for RIGHT flank which was pressed back owing to Brigade on the RIGHT not advancing. This flank was quickly barraged by our guns. 200,000 rds fired 31st to 1st inst. Lt WOOD reported to F.A. suffering from gas. Evacuated. Guns at JUNCTION BUILDINGS relieved by 7th M.G. Coy. Gas shells much used by enemy.	
	2/8/17		Company in line with 12 guns harrassing fire continued.	
	3/8/17		All Barrage gun positions held by 2 men per gun only & N.C.O. & Officer per Group. Lt LENTHWAITE moved up to line with one gun with the object of strengthening line after minor offensive.	
	4/8/17		Normal conditions. Shelling active on both sides. Gas shells much used by enemy.	
	5/8/17		Condition normal. 8 pm enemy counter attacked on HOLLEBEKE. S.O.S. sent up on RIGHT of our Division. All guns in line including those at Adv Coy H.Qrs. were brought into action. Attack unsuccessful.	

A5834 Wt. W4973/M687 750,000 8/16 D. D. & L. Ltd. Forms/C.2118/13.

Instructions regarding War Diaries and Intelligence Summaries are contained in F. S. Regs., Part II. and the Staff Manual respectively. Title pages will be prepared in manuscript.

WAR DIARY
or
INTELLIGENCE SUMMARY.
(Erase heading not required.)

Army Form C. 2118.

Place	Date	Hour	Summary of Events and Information	Remarks and references to Appendices
	6/8/17		Conditions normal. Gas shells very much used by enemy	
	7/8/17		O.C. 63rd M. G. Coy met O.C. 58 M. G. Coy and 246 M G Coy at Bde. H.Q.	
			Relief arranged. O.C. 58 M. G. Coy made responsible for relief of	
			RIGHT Bde Sector by D.M.G.O.	
	8/8/17		Arrival of 63rd M. G Coy for relieving 8.20pm	
			Coy moved with Transport to BAILLEUL	
	9/8/17		1 AM Relief complete. Sections in line moved to Transport Lines.	
			Then to BAILLEUL at 6. am.	
	10/8/17		Company moved by train to ZART near LUMBRES.	
			Company Transport moved with 56 - 246th M G Coy + 58 F.A. to STAPLE.	
	11/8/17		Company at ZART	
			Transport lines moved to ARQUES.	
	12/8/17		Company at ZART.	
			Transport finished arriving at ZART at 4.20 pm.	
			No casualties to Transport during march	
	13/8/17		Company at ZART. Cleaning + refitting	
	14/8/17		Company at ZART. Cleaning + refitting	
	15/8/17		Company at ZART 2 Sections firing on range. 1 Section range fatigue	
			1 Section cleaning remainder of Coy Belts + refilling	

A5834 Wt. W4973/M687 750,000 8/16 D. D. & L. Ltd. Forms/C.2118/13.

Instructions regarding War Diaries and Intelligence Summaries are contained in F. S. Regs., Part II. and the Staff Manual respectively. Title pages will be prepared in manuscript.

WAR DIARY
or
INTELLIGENCE SUMMARY.
(Erase heading not required.)

Army Form C. 2118.

Place	Date	Hour	Summary of Events and Information	Remarks and references to Appendices
	16/8/17		Company at LART. Range firing practice	
	17/8/17		Company at LART. Range practise.	
	18/8/17		Company at LART. Infantry Drill, Brigade Sports, General Holiday	
	19/8/17		Company at LART. Church Parade	
	20/8/17		Company at LART. Sections on Range Transport practising Pack Mules on Route March. G.O.C. Division. O.C.s 57 & 58 M.G. Coy attended Demonstration at CAMIERS by H.Q. M.G. School	
	21/8/17		Company at LART. 1 Section on Tactical Exercises. Remainder on Range	
	22/8/17		Company at LART. O.C. attended Tactical Exercise by 9th Cheshire Regt One Section taking part. Remainder of Coy on Range practices with pack mules &c.	
	23/8/17		Company at LART. Company on Range. Lt. J.H. OLIVER THOMPSON appointed O.C. 120th M.G. Company.	
	24/8/17		Company at LART. Rehearsal of C. in C. Inspection.	
	25/8/17		Company at LART C. in C. Inspection <u>Dress</u> Bde in Belt, Sidearms & Rifle.	
	26/8/17		Company at LART Section Parades. Cricket Match v 57th F.A.	

A5834 Wt. W4973/M687 750,000 8/16 D. D. & L. Ltd. Forms/C.2118/13.

Instructions regarding War Diaries and Intelligence Summaries are contained in F. S. Regs., Part II. and the Staff Manual respectively. Title pages will be prepared in manuscript.

WAR DIARY
or
INTELLIGENCE SUMMARY.
(Erase heading not required.)

Army Form C. 2118.

Place	Date	Hour	Summary of Events and Information	Remarks and references to Appendices
	27/8/17		Company at LART Section parade. Route March. Transport moved to ARQUES	
	28/8/17		Company moved to BAILLEUL by train from WIZERNES. then marched to 1 mile EAST of WESTOUTRE Transport moved to STAPLES.	
	29/8/17		Company arrived at WESTOUTRE area 2.0 am. Rested during day.	
	30/8/17		Company at WESTOUTRE. Section parade. Route March	
	2/9/17		Infantry Drill. Route March. Lecture by D.M.G.O. at 2.30 pm	
			for W. [illegible] Lt	

A5834 Wt. W4973/M687 750,000 8/16 D. D. & L. Ltd. Forms/C.2118/13.

Instructions regarding War Diaries and Intelligence Summaries are contained in F. S. Regs., Part II. and the Staff Manual respectively. Title Pages will be prepared in manuscript.

WAR DIARY
or
INTELLIGENCE SUMMARY
(Erase heading not required.)

58 M G Coy for September 1917

Army Form C. 2118

Vol 19

Place	Date	Hour	Summary of Events and Information	Remarks and references to Appendices
WESTOUTRE	1/9/17		Brigade Training	
	2/9/17		Church parades, Kit Inspections.	
	3/9/17		Gas exercise, Gunning practice Machine Gun Drill, Advanced Gun Drill. Barrage Drill. Tactical Scheme.	
	4/9/17		Route March. N.C.O.s Lecture on sending in reports.	
	5/9/17		Company Tactical Scheme	
	6/9/17		Gas exercise, Infantry Drill Map reading Judging distance Gun Drill	
	7/9/17		Gas exercise, Infantry Drill, Direct overhead Covering fire. Overhauling of limbers	
	8/9/17		Gas exercise, musketry practice Lecture for Junior N.C.O.s on present forms of German Defence. Tactical exercise, Range taking	
	9/9/17		Infantry Drill, Route March, Carrying all gun equipment over Rough Country. [illegible] parade	

1875 Wt. W593/826 1,000,000 4/15 J.B.C. & A. A.D.S.S./Forms/C. 2118.

Instructions regarding War Diaries and Intelligence Summaries are contained in F. S. Regs., Part II. and the Staff Manual respectively. Title Pages will be prepared in manuscript.

WAR DIARY
or
INTELLIGENCE SUMMARY
(Erase heading not required.)

Army Form C. 2118

Place	Date	Hour	Summary of Events and Information	Remarks and references to Appendices
WESTOUTRE	10/9/17		Company marched to KEMMEL area at N.10.c.5.5.	
N.10.c.5.5.	11/9/17		Cleaning of Guns, Ammunition Belts & Belt Boxes. Gun Teams proceeded to line & took over from the 63rd M. G. Coy.	
	12/9/17		Company in line Line reconnoitered by all Officers	
	13/9/17		Company in line	
	14/9/17		Company in line	
	15/9/17		Company relieved in line by 56th M. G. Coy.	
	16/9/17		Company at rest near KEMMEL C.O.s conference with G. O. C. Brigade.	
	17/9/17		Company participated in practice attack with [illegible] Reconnoissance of line by O.C.	
	18/9/17		Company at rest. Reconnoissance of line, by O.C. & Officers	

1875 Wt. W593/826 1,000,000 4/15 J.B.C. & A. A.D.S.S./Forms/C. 2118.

Instructions regarding War Diaries and Intelligence Summaries are contained in F. S. Regs., Part II. and the Staff Manual respectively. Title Pages will be prepared in manuscript.

WAR DIARY
or
INTELLIGENCE SUMMARY
(Erase heading not required.)

Army Form C. 2118

Place	Date	Hour	Summary of Events and Information	Remarks and references to Appendices
N.10.C.5.5	19/9/17		Company moved into the assembly positions in the evening meeting the Infantry on the way to the line. 4 Teams moved into Barrage position & 2 were attached to 97 M. G. Coy.	
	20/9/17		Company in the 2nd Army advance excellent weather conditions Guns moving over with Infantry, 2 in rear of Infantry. 2 moved to a strong point & 4 moved into the British old Front Line after attack. ZERO Hour 5.40 am. Pte CHATER distinguishing himself by single handed attacking 2 enemy machine guns in action, killing one & taking 3 prisoners. L/Cpl MITCHELL by his determined efforts & splendid work on the LEFT flank of the Brigade communicated successfully.	
	21/9/17		Company in the line with 14 Guns. Casualties reported 4 killed 5 wounded	
	22/9/17		Company in the line with 13 Guns. Relief by 46th M.G. Coy started at dusk. Sgt BOYD. D.C.M. killed.	
	23/9/17		Company at rest less 4 Gun Teams who owing to casualties to incoming relief were not relieved. Weather fine [illegible] attack.	
	24/9/17		Overhauling of guns & spare parts. Repacking of limbers.	

1875 Wt. W593/826 1,000,000 4/15 J.B.C. & A. A.D.S.S./Forms/C. 2118.

Instructions regarding War Diaries and Intelligence Summaries are contained in F. S. Regs., Part II. and the Staff Manual respectively. Title pages will be prepared in manuscript.

WAR DIARY
or
INTELLIGENCE SUMMARY.
(Erase heading not required.)

Army Form C. 2118.

Place	Date	Hour	Summary of Events and Information	Remarks and references to Appendices
N.10.C.5.5.	25/9/17		Company Inspected by G.O.C. 1st Brigade.	
	26/9/17		Route March, Overhauling of limbers. Cleaning of Belts, Belt Boxes & ammunition.	
	27/9/17		Infantry Drill, Cleaning of guns overhauling of spare parts. N.C.O.s revolver practice.	
	28/9/17		Arm & Squad Drill, Gun Drill, Judging Distance	
	29/9/17		Infantry Drill, Gun Drill, Stoppages.	
	30/9/17		Church parades.	

for [signature] Lt.
[stamp illegible] CORPS

A5834 Wt. W4973/M687 750,000 8/16 D. D. & L. Ltd. Forms/C.2118/13.

Army Form C. 2118.

WAR DIARY
or
INTELLIGENCE SUMMARY.
(*Erase heading not required.*)

Instructions regarding War Diaries and Intelligence Summaries are contained in F. S. Regs., Part II. and the Staff Manual respectively. Title pages will be prepared in manuscript.

Place	Date	Hour	Summary of Events and Information	Remarks and references to Appendices
	1/10/17		Gun positions taken over from 57 M. G. Coy Four Gun Team relieved O.C. 58 Company moved up to HILL 60 and took over charge of LEFT BRIGADE SECTOR Organisation of Machine Gun Defence Scheme of 19th Division started to be put into effect: Scheme as follows	
SHREWSBURY FOREST	2/10/17		Machine Gun Defence, LEFT SECTOR, will from now on be referred to: Twelve Guns in the line.	
YPRES SALIENT	3/10/17		Four Guns of 57 Coy, Two Guns of 58 Coy moved up into position on Pack Mules during the evening to Barrage positions dug during the day. These guns were to assist the attack of the Division on the left. Back areas & tracks were heavily shelled during the day. Five casualties occurred on the journey.	
	4/10/17		Machine Guns on the LEFT SECTOR assisted the advance of the 37th Division by Direct & Indirect Fire on the RIGHT flank of the 37th Division. Fire was opened at ZERO plus three minutes and was kept up for two hours at the average rate of 60 rounds per minute. From 6. 0 am throughout the day the Barrage positions were heavily shelled. At 6.0 am an English marked plane thought to be German, flew over the line at a very low altitude.	

A5834 Wt. W4973/M687 750,000 8/16 D. D. & L. Ltd. Forms/C.2118/13.

Instructions regarding War Diaries and Intelligence Summaries are contained in F. S. Regs., Part II. and the Staff Manual respectively. Title pages will be prepared in manuscript.

WAR DIARY or INTELLIGENCE SUMMARY.

(Erase heading not required.)

58 Machine Gun Company for month of October 1917

Army Form C. 2118.

Vol 20

Place	Date	Hour	Summary of Events and Information	Remarks and references to Appendices
	5/10/17		Company in the line, with 8 guns of 58 Company and 8 guns of 57 Company. Barrage positions moved to alternative emplacement. 6 Guns relieved	
	6/10/17		Company in the line with 8 guns	
	7/10/17		Company in the line with 8 guns	
	8/10/17		Company in the line with 10 guns. 57 Company with six guns (two Barrage Guns taken over from 57 Coy during the afternoon) Division warned to be ready to move forward in case of enemy opposition slackening. First objective ZANDVOORDE RIDGE.	
	9/10/17		Company in the line. O.C. 58 Company handed over command of the LEFT Sector to O.C. 57 Coy. Lt SMELTZER left at C.H.Q. to represent Company	
	10/10/17		Company in the line. 7.30 am relief of 4 Gun Teams at Barrage positions started from Transport Line. Strength 1 N.C.O + 5 men. Six teams started from Transport Line at 2 pm to relieve teams in the line. All personnel were conveyed in limbers	
	11/10/17		Company in the line. Relief for the 10th inst completed by 10 am	
	12/10/17		Company in the line	

A5834 Wt. W4973/M687 750,000 8/16 D. D. & L. Ltd. Forms/C.2118/13.

Army Form C. 2118.

Instructions regarding War Diaries and Intelligence Summaries are contained in F. S. Regs., Part II. and the Staff Manual respectively. Title pages will be prepared in manuscript.

WAR DIARY
or
INTELLIGENCE SUMMARY.
(Erase heading not required.)

Place	Date	Hour	Summary of Events and Information	Remarks and references to Appendices
	13.10.17		½ Coy in line	JCB
	14.10.17		½ Coy in line Relief of Teams in line	JCB
	15.10.17		½ Coy in line	JCB
	16.10.17		½ Coy in line	JCB
	17.10.17		½ Coy in line. O.C. 58 takes command of LEFT DIV: M.G. Defence	JCB
	18.10.17		½ Coy in line Relief of teams in line	JCB
	19.10.17		½ Coy in line	JCB
	20.10.17		½ Coy in line — Enemy Shelling — quiet.	JCB
	21.10.17		½ Coy in line — Instructions received re coming offensive on NORTH of sec 15 - OC 57 reconnoitred positions	JCB
	22.10.17		½ Coy in line — Preparation for barrage positions started. OC reconnoitred positions for 57 M.G. Coy } Relief of teams in line	JCB
	23.10.17		Working Parties of 57 & 58 M.G. Coys move up to chosen positions with material } [illegible] ½ Coy in line. OC 58 M.G.C conducted preparation for 6 emplacements for barrage for 57 M.G. Coy }	JCB
	24.10.17		½ Coy in line. Working party under 2/Lt DENT moved out having completed 4 emplacements for barrage { Enemy Shelling increased	JCB
	25.10.17		½ Coy in line. 4 teams move up to prepared positions for barrage for coming offensive on LEFT & N of DIV: OC 58 handed over to OC 57 Command of LEFT Sector	
	26.10.17		Weather bad. 10 Teams in the line. 4 Barrage teams assisted in operation on RIGHT FLANK of DIV on LEFT by barrage 2000x N. of ZANDVOORDE	JCB
	27.10.17		½ Coy in line — Relieved. 2 Barrage teams moved to original position & come under command of 57 M.G. Coy again	JCB
	28.10.17		½ Coy in line Enemy Shelling decreasing.	JCB
	29.10.17		½ Coy in line. G.O.C. Brigade inspected Transport and Camp. Satisfactory Report	JCB
	30.10.17		½ Coy in line — Salvage party D.M.G.O. Inspected Camp	JCB
	31/10/17		½ Coy in line — Relieved.	JCB

J C Bramhall Capt
COMD: No. 58 COY. MACHINE GUN CORPS.

A5834 Wt. W4973/M687 750,000 8/16 D. D. & L. Ltd. Forms/C.2118/13.

Instructions regarding War Diaries and Intelligence Summaries are contained in F. S. Regs., Part II. and the Staff Manual respectively. Title Pages will be prepared in manuscript.

1.12.17

WAR DIARY
or
INTELLIGENCE SUMMARY
(Erase heading not required.)

58 M.G. Coy for Month Nov. 1917

Vol 22

Army Form C. 2118.

Place	Date	Hour	Summary of Events and Information	Remarks and references to Appendices
VIERSTRAAT	Nov. 1.		½ Coy in line – All teams relieved	JCB
	" 2.		½ Coy in line – Front Quiet – O.C. 58 M.G. Coy took command of LEFT DIV. M.G. Sector.	JCB
	" 3.		½ Coy in line – Orders for BARRAGE to be laid down for operations to take place on the 7th inst received	JCB
	" 4.		½ Coy in line –	JCB
	" 5.		½ Coy in line – All arrangements re barrage for 7th inst cancelled. – Front Quiet – Gas shell struck dug-out on HILL 60 causing 3 casualties	JCB
	" 6		½ Coy in line Attack at 6 AM on LEFT – NORTH of DIV. FRONT brought retaliation by enemy artillery on communications to Front Line – All teams relieved – Conference at SPOILBANK of relieving M.G. Coys.	JCB
	" 7		½ Coy in line – O.C. 112 MG Coy visited O.C. 58 M.G. Coy at HILL 60 to complete arrangements re relief of LEFT SECTOR.	JCB
	" 8		½ Coy in line – 57 & 58 M.G. Coys. were relieved in the line by the 112 M.G. Coy Relief started at 5 p.m. completed at 10 p.m. less One Officer who reported personally relieved by 4 AM 9.10.17	JCB
STRAZEELE	" 9		Coy marched from VIERSTRAAT to STRAZEELE no casualties	JCB
	" 10		Conference of COs at Bde HQ on Training and Sports during the Period out of the line.	JCB
EBBLINGHEM	" 11		Coy marched from STRAZEELE to 1 mile SOUTH of EBBLINGHEM no casualties.	JCB
	" 12		Coy Parade – redistribution of reinforcements into the Company – Cleaning up	JCB
	" 13		Coy Training Programme started. P.&D. Arms Drill 50% M.G. Drill & Firing 50% First week	JCB
	" 14 to 20		Coy Training – Steady Drill – P.T. – M.G. Drill & Firing – Football during afternoon – 44 men playing per day Range in construction	JCB

2449 Wt. W14957/M90 750,000 1/16 J.B.C. & A. Forms/C.2118/12.

Army Form C. 2118.

Instructions regarding War Diaries and Intelligence Summaries are contained in F. S. Regs., Part II. and the Staff Manual respectively. Title Pages will be prepared in manuscript.

WAR DIARY
or
INTELLIGENCE SUMMARY
(Erase heading not required.)

Place	Date	Hour	Summary of Events and Information	Remarks and references to Appendices
	Nov 21.		Coy Training. Coy Arms Drill under C.S.M. Guard Mounting practice Lecture to N.C.O's Map "Drawing and copying". Digging Fatigue on Range	JCB
EBBLINGHEM	22.		Coy Training S.D. Arms Drill under C.S.M. 2 hrs. Sections under Officers 2 hours Lecture Barrage Chart.	JCB
	23.		Coy Training S.D. Arms Drill under C.S.M. 2 hours Sections under Officers 2 hours	JCB
	24		Coy Training. Squad Arms Drill under Section Officers Digging Fatigue Inspection of transport by Brigadier	JCB
	25.		Church Parade	JCB
	26		Coy Training under Section Officers Range completed.	JCB
	27.		Coy Training Examination of ~~[illegible]~~ Sections by C.O in short scheme	JCB
	28		Baths. Coy Training Range Firing 25 x. Lecture to N.C.Os & Men Cleaning of Rifle	JCB
	29		Coy Training under Section Officers Limber Drill	JCB
	30		Coy Training under Section Officers	JCB

2449 Wt. W14957/M90 750,000 1/16 J.B.C. & A. Forms/C.2118/12.

58th Machine Gun Coy
19th Division

Instructions regarding War Diaries and Intelligence Summaries are contained in F. S. Regs., Part II. and the Staff Manual respectively. Title Pages will be prepared in manuscript.

WAR DIARY
or
INTELLIGENCE SUMMARY
(Erase heading not required.)

Confidential
58 M G Coy
for month of December 1917

Army Form C. 2118.

Vol 22.

Place	Date	Hour	Summary of Events and Information	Remarks and references to Appendices
EBBLINGHEM	1/12/17		Company Training	
	2/12/17		Company Training	
	3/12/17		General GLASGOW expressed his intention of inspecting the Section training for the Divisional Competition.	
	4/12/17		Section training for the Divisional Competition inspected by D.M.G.O. General GLASGOW being unable to inspect. Company mounted a Brigade Guard.	
	5/12/17		Company at rest.	
	6/12/17		Company Football Match 1 + 2 Sections versus 3 + 4 Sections	
	7/12/17		Company entrained at ARQUES detrained at BEAUMETZ les LISLORGES Company on detraining duties during night.	
BLAIRVILLE	8/12/17		Company marched from BLAIRVILLE to GOMIECOURT.	
GOMIECOURT	9/12/17		Company marched from GOMIECOURT to ETRICOURT.	
ETRICOURT	10/12/17		Company at ETRICOURT. O.C. & Officers reconnoitred the line.	
	11/12/17		Company less Transport moved from ETRICOURT to the line to relieve 71 M G Coy. 16 Guns 1 N.C.O + 4 men being the strength of each team Relief started at 5 p.m.	

2449 Wt. W14957/M90 750,000 1/16 J.B.C. & A. Forms/C.2118/12.

Army Form C. 2118.

WAR DIARY
or
INTELLIGENCE SUMMARY
(Erase heading not required.)

Instructions regarding War Diaries and Intelligence Summaries are contained in F. S. Regs., Part II. and the Staff Manual respectively. Title Pages will be prepared in manuscript.

Place	Date	Hour	Summary of Events and Information	Remarks and references to Appendices
RIBECOURT	12/12/17		Company in the line. 16 Guns, 4 Officers. Relief completed by 4.0 am	
	13/12/17		Company in the line 16 Guns, 4 Officers. O.C. tour of Guns. Whole DIVISION stood to 6.0 am to 8.30 am. Transport moved forward FINS area.	
	14/12/17		Company in line. 16 Guns, 4 Officers.	
	15/12/17		Company in line. 16 Guns, 4 Officers. O.C's tour of RIGHT BATTALION. Right Section with D.M.G.O.	
	16/12/17		Company in the line 16 Guns. 4 Officers. O.C's Tour of LEFT BATTALION RIGHT Sector	
	17/12/17		Company in line. 16 Guns - 4 Officers. O.C. reconnoitred line on LEFT of DIVISION and LEFT Bde Sector.	
	18/12/17		Company in line. 16 Guns 4 Officers. O.C. reconnoitred new line on RIGHT of COUILLET WOOD. Conference with G.O.C. Brigade.	
	19/12/17		Company in line with 16 Guns 4 Officers. Orders received with reference to the reorganisation of 14 Machine Guns of the Division. Conference between O.C. 58 + 57 M. Gun Coys. Owing to severe frost all Guns were ordered to fire during the night on Special Targets. Transport moved forward to HAVRINCOURT WOOD	
	20/12/17		Divisional Machine Gun Defence. 2 Groups of 24 Guns RIGHT + LEFT Group commanded by O.C. 58 + O.C. 57 M.G. Coys respectively.	

2449 Wt. W14957/M90 750,000 1/16 J.B.C. & A. Forms/C.2118/12.

Army Form C. 2118.

WAR DIARY
or
INTELLIGENCE SUMMARY
(Erase heading not required.)

Instructions regarding War Diaries and Intelligence Summaries are contained in F. S. Regs., Part II. and the Staff Manual respectively. Title Pages will be prepared in manuscript.

Place	Date	Hour	Summary of Events and Information	Remarks and references to Appendices
	20/12/17		Each Company in the Division having 12 Guns in the line. one Section out of the line at Transport Lines.	
	21/12/17		Company in line. Reorganised.	
	22/12/17		Company in line 12 Guns	
	23/12/17		Company in line 12 Guns	
	24/12/17		Company in line 12 Guns. Line quiet.	
	25/12/17		Company in line 12 Guns Line quiet	
	26/12/17		Company in line 12 Guns Line quiet.	
	27/12/17		Company in line 12 Guns. 12 O.Rs from 9th Welsh Regt 20 ORs from 6th Wiltshire Regt attached to company by Brigade orders. Thick snow.	
	28/12/17		Company in the Line 12 Guns. O.C., made a tour of the RIGHT Group with the Divisional General and D.M.G.O. F.G.C.M. held in the case of No 15191 Pte MONK. W + 6221 Pte BURCH. H.E. Thick snow, very clear atmosphere. Line quiet. 10 men bathed at Company H.Q.	

Instructions regarding War Diaries and Intelligence Summaries are contained in F. S. Regs., Part II. and the Staff Manual respectively. Title Pages will be prepared in manuscript.

WAR DIARY
or
INTELLIGENCE SUMMARY
(Erase heading not required.)

Army Form C. 2118.

Place	Date	Hour	Summary of Events and Information	Remarks and references to Appendices
	29/12/17		Company in the line with 12 guns, day quiet. [initials]	
	30/12/17		Company in the line with 12 guns. day very quiet. [initials]	
	31/12/17		Company in the line with 12 guns. 6.30 am Enemy attack on Right of Divisional Sector. Guns covering that front, fired on the S.O.S. Division on the Right, shelled heavily during the day. Night quiet. Remainder of Company paraded for the promulgation of sentence on Pt. MONK, 58th Machine Gun Company of 42 days F P No 2 & £1 fine. [initials]	
			John B [illegible] Lt for OC 58th Machine Gun Coy 19th Division	

2449 Wt. W14957/M90 750,000 1/16 J.B.C. & A. Forms/C.2118/12.

58 COMPANY
28.2.18
MG418
MACHINE GUN CORPS

58th. Infantry Brigade

From
O.C. 58 Machine Gun Coy

Confidential

War Diary
of
58 Machine Gun Company

from 1.2.18 to 28.2.18.
(Volume No 4)

W B Dent Lieut
COMD. No 58 COY. MACHINE GUN CORPS.

Instructions regarding War Diaries and Intelligence Summaries are contained in F. S. Regs., Part II. and the Staff Manual respectively. Title Pages will be prepared in manuscript.

WAR DIARY
or
INTELLIGENCE SUMMARY
(Erase heading not required.)

58 MG Coy
For January 1918

Vol 23

Army Form C. 2118.

Place	Date	Hour	Summary of Events and Information	Remarks and references to Appendices
	1/1/18		12 Machine Guns in the line in COULLIET WOOD Sector. Enemy very quiet & weather cold.	
	2/1/18		Machine Guns being formed into Batteries in & near the Support line Enemy quiet	
	3/1/18		Reconnoitering of all Ground by Company Officers for sites.	
	4/1/18		Section 1 vacated position in front line and took up a position as "A" Battery. Enemy shelling front line.	
	5/1/18		Teams busy preparing Battery positions. Snow falling heavily. Enemy quiet. Signallers from Battalions attached.	
	6/1/18		4 Teams took up Battery positions. Telephone wires being laid out to Batteries.	
	7/1/18		12 Guns still in the line. Day ~~quiet~~ fine & enemy aeroplanes active.	
	8/1/18		Enemy quiet. Inter Section relief.	
	9/1/18		4 Guns move to take up Battery positions. Enemy shelling heavily	
	10/1/18		S.O.S. seen on RIGHT of Sector. Right Battery Groups opened fire on S.O.S. lines until situation cleared	
	11/1/18		Enemy aeroplane activity engaged by our M. Guns	

2449 Wt. W14957/M90 750,000 1/16 J.B.C. & A. Forms/C.2118/12.

Instructions regarding War Diaries and Intelligence Summaries are contained in F. S. Regs., Part II. and the Staff Manual respectively. Title Pages will be prepared in manuscript.

WAR DIARY
or
INTELLIGENCE SUMMARY
(Erase heading not required.)

Army Form C. 2118.

Place	Date	Hour	Summary of Events and Information	Remarks and references to Appendices
	12/1/18		Inter team relief. Enemy quiet.	
	13/1/18		Battery positions now occupied. Disposition of guns now being, 3 Battery positions + 4 front line guns.	
	14/1/18		Weather broken, heavy rains + trenches impassible. Reserve areas heavily shelled.	
	15/1/18		Situation quiet.	
	16/1/18		Inter team relief. Back areas heavily shelled	
	17/1/18		Enemy active. Harrassing fire by our M. Guns in conjunction with Artillery to hinder enemy relief.	
	18/1/18		Morning clear, enemy planes active, back areas heavily shelled.	
	19/1/18		Day clear, much enemy movement reported by our sentries. Artillery quiet.	
	20/1/18		Inter team relief. A large number of Gas Shells distributed on the whole sector. Enemy artillery very active.	
	21/1/18		Observation excellent; much enemy aircraft + artillery activity presumably registering on special targets. Our S.O.S. seen on right of Sector + barrage by M. Guns + Artillery put down.	

2449 Wt. W14957/M90 750,000 1/16 J.B.C. & A. Forms/C.2118/12.

Army Form C. 2118.

Instructions regarding War Diaries and Intelligence Summaries are contained in F. S. Regs., Part II. and the Staff Manual respectively. Title Pages will be prepared in manuscript.

WAR DIARY
or
INTELLIGENCE SUMMARY

(Erase heading not required.)

Place	Date	Hour	Summary of Events and Information	Remarks and references to Appendices
	21/1/18		Enemy also put down barrage between our front & Support line.	
	22/1/18		Development of Trench Mortar activity on our front line. No action followed.	
	23/1/18		Increasing enemy activity with Gas shells. Back area heavily shelled. 4 Teams interchanging with Company on Right Sector.	
	24/1/18		Inter team relief. Enemy very quiet.	
	25/1/18		Enemy aeroplane activity. Artillery quiet.	
	26/1/18		Weather misty. No artillery activity	
	27/1/18		4 Teams interchanged with teams on Right Sector	
	28/1/18		Enemy very active with aircraft & balloons up. Intermittent shelling all day.	
	29/1/18		Intermittent shelling all day.	
	30/1/18		Day fairly quiet.	
	31/1/18		4 Teams interchanged with teams on right Sector	

COMD. No. [illegible] COY. MACHINE GUN CORPS.

Confidential

Instructions regarding War Diaries and Intelligence Summaries are contained in F. S. Regs., Part II. and the Staff Manual respectively. Title Pages will be prepared in manuscript.

WAR DIARY
or
INTELLIGENCE SUMMARY
(Erase heading not required.)

For February 1918

Army Form C. 2118.

Place	Date	Hour	Summary of Events and Information	Remarks and references to Appendices
	1/2/18		12 Guns in the line. Right Sector reconnoitred by O.C. Right Group. WBD	
	2/2/18		12 Guns in the line. Positions of 2 guns changed WBD Night Firing carried out by the Company with greater vigour. WBD	
	3/2/18		12 Guns in the line. Weather misty. guns firing during day. WBD	
	4/2/18		12 Guns in the line. Enemy quiet all day. WBD Relief of 4 Teams by Section in reserve. WBD	
	5/2/18		12 Guns in the line. Enemy quiet. WBD	
	6/2/18		12 Guns in the line. Enemy Artillery active. WBD	
	7/2/18		12 Guns in the line. S.O.S. went up on our left at early morning WBD 4 teams stood by until daylight. WBD	
	8/2/18		12 Guns in the line. Enemy very quiet. WBD	
	9/2/18		12 Guns in the line. Enemy very quiet. WBD	
	10/2/18		12 Guns in the line. Enemy quiet by day. Heavy shelling at night. WBD	
	11/2/18		12 Guns in the line. Enemy quiet. Heavy shelling at night. WBD Reconnoitering of line by O.C. relieving Company WBD	
	12/2/18		12 Guns in the line. Enemy very quiet. WBD Reconnoitering of line by Officer of 188 + 189 M.G. Coys who are relieving. WBD	

Instructions regarding War Diaries and Intelligence Summaries are contained in F. S. Regs., Part II. and the Staff Manual respectively. Title Pages will be prepared in manuscript.

WAR DIARY
or
INTELLIGENCE SUMMARY
(Erase heading not required.)

Army Form C. 2118.

Place	Date	Hour	Summary of Events and Information	Remarks and references to Appendices
	13/2/18		Relief of 9 teams by the 189th M. G. Coy. Completed by 11.30 pm WBD	
			Transport of the Company moved to new camp at BEAULENCOURT. WBD	
	14/2/18		Relief of remaining 3 gun teams. WBD	
			O.C. Company after witnessing Tank demonstration at BRAY, proceeded to CAMIERS on a course.	
LE TRANSLOY	15/2/18		Company in camp resting. WBD	
	16/2/18		Cleaning of guns material. Conference of O.C. Company with Battalion Commander Col. WINSER. D.S.O. WBD	
			Lt SMELTZER transferred to 44th M.G. Coy Lt A.D.D. BONNER arrived	
	17/2/18		Church parades WBD	
	18/2/18		Training according to Battalion programme WBD	
	19/2/18			
	20/2/18		Training according to Battalion programme. WBD	
			Lt DENT + 2/Lts CUNDALL + MORRIS proceeded to BOULOGNE on Camouflage course.	
	21/2/18			
	23/2/18		Training according to Battalion programme. WBD	
	24/2/18		Church parades. WBD	
	25/2/18			
	26/2/18		Training according to Battalion programme. WBD	

2449 Wt. W14957/M90 750,000 1/16 J.B.C. & A. Forms/C.2118/12.

Army Form C. 2118.

WAR DIARY
or
INTELLIGENCE SUMMARY
(Erase heading not required.)

Instructions regarding War Diaries and Intelligence Summaries are contained in F. S. Regs., Part II. and the Staff Manual respectively. Title Pages will be prepared in manuscript.

Place	Date	Hour	Summary of Events and Information	Remarks and references to Appendices
	27/7/18		Battalion moved in conjunction with Divl scheme for manning 3rd Line near ROYALCOURT. WBD	
	28/7/18		Training according to Battalion programme. WBD	

WBDent Lieut
COMD. No. 53 ... MACHINE GUN CORPS.

2449 Wt. W14957/M90 750,000 1/16 J.B.C. & A. Forms/C.2118/12.

www.ingramcontent.com/pod-product-compliance
Lightning Source LLC
Chambersburg PA
CBHW081441160426
43193CB00013B/2349

* 9 7 8 1 4 7 4 5 1 1 4 3 8 *